Float by Faith

Lisa Buffaloe

Float by Faith
Copyright 2022 Lisa Buffaloe (updated 071423)
John 15:11 Publications, Florence, AL 35630

All rights reserved. No part of this book may be reproduced or transmitted in any way, form, or by any means, electronic or mechanical—including photocopying, recording, or by any information storage and retrieval system— except brief quotations in printed reviews, without permission of the author.

Visit the author's website at https://lisabuffaloe.com

ISBN - 978-1-957715-07-0 (E-Book)
ISBN - 978-1-957715-08-7 (Paperback)
ISBN - 978-1-957715-09-4 (Hardback)

Cover design: Lisa Buffaloe

Printed in the United States of America

Soli Deo Gloria

Contents

Float by Faith	1
Stormy weather	24
Downdrafts	76
Staying in service	97
Powered up	126
Fueled and fired up	145
About the author	166
Books by Lisa Buffaloe	166
Bible credits and Bibliography	168

Float by Faith

During hot air balloon festivals, brightly colored balloons of various shapes and sizes fill the sky. Air inside the bags, or envelopes, is heated by an open flame which makes the envelope buoyant. Sandbags and ropes keep a balloon on the ground until ready to fly. Once untethered, they become airborne and float free in the sky.

I would love to float in clear skies, serene, carefree, and untethered from life's difficulties. However, the worries of this world often weigh me down.

This quote by Lettie Cowman challenged me, "It is a sign of weakness to always worry and fret, question everything, and mistrust everyone. Can anything be gained by it? Don't we only make ourselves unfit for action, and separate our minds from the ability to make wise decisions? We simply sink in our struggles when we could float by faith."[1]

Doesn't floating by faith sound wonderful?

I like the visual that gives; however, I wonder what

ties us down -- anxiety, frustration, worries, news reports, unending distractions, health issues, life issues, and fear of so very many things?

Then I wondered, what fuels us – do we allow God, and His Holy Spirit, to fill us with His joy and peace?

Are we willing to drop the sandbags that tether, hinder, and hold us from flying free?

And, how can we navigate over obstacles and through life's storms?

Isaiah 40:31 tells us, "those who wait for the Lord [who expect, look for, and hope in Him] will gain new strength and renew their power; they will lift up their wings [and rise up close to God] like eagles [rising toward the sun]; they will run and not become weary, they will walk and not grow tired (AMP).

Warren Wiersbe wrote, "God promises to help us fly. There are times in our lives when the only solution is to fly—to rise above the problems of life and soar over them. God wants to make eagles out of us, but sometimes we prefer to crawl like ants. What a tragedy! God is able to lift you above those difficult circumstances that have trapped you. This doesn't mean you ignore or forget them; it means that you rise above them and get a heavenly perspective. The eagle is able to fly miles up in the sky—and when you do that, the things on earth start to look much smaller. Yes, my friend, God promises to make you fly."[2]

Do you long to live free and fly untethered and unhindered, floating through life?

If the answer is yes, the first step is to get off the ground by accepting the free gift of God's grace offered through His Son, Jesus Christ. God loved the world SO much that He sent His only Son to offer salvation to all who will believe in Christ as Savior.

Our "goodness" can never be enough to enter the presence of a Holy God. No matter what we do, how much we work to be "good" and do "good" to others, that will never be enough to compensate for our sin, the wrong things we have done. For just one little, tiny sin will keep us from standing in front of a pure and holy God and to gain entrance to heaven.

Our loving God preplanned our rescue before we were born and before we would ever sin. He had a plan in place to give us the choice, and the chance, to be saved and with Him forever. Jesus Christ willingly sacrificed His life in our place so that *His* worthiness and *His* perfection would pay for our unworthiness and imperfection.

"There was no other good enough to pay the price of sin; He only could unlock the gate of heaven and let us in." ~ Cecil F. Alexander

Alexander Maclaren wrote, "Without Jesus Christ, we are orphans in a fatherless world. Without Him our wearied and yet unsatisfied eyes have only trifles and trials and trash to look at. Without Him, we are dead while we live. He and He only can give us back a Father and renew in us the spirit of sons. He and only He can satisfy our eyes with the sight that is purity and restfulness and joy. He and He only can breathe life into our death. Oh, let Him do it for you! He comes to us with all these gifts in His hands, for He comes to give us Himself, and in Himself are all that lonely hearts and wearied eyes and dead souls can ever need. All are yours, if you are Christ's. All our yours, if He is yours. And He is yours, if by faith and love you make yourself Him and Him your own."[3]

Have you accepted the offer of God's grace? Christ will never force or push; He holds out His nail-scarred, loving hand for all who will receive His forgiveness, grace, mercy, and salvation. "For everyone has sinned; we all fall short of God's glorious standard. Yet God, in his grace, freely makes us right in his sight. He did this through Christ Jesus when he freed us from the penalty for our sins. For God presented Jesus as the sacrifice for sin. People are made right with God when they believe that Jesus sacrificed his life, shedding his blood. ... God did this to demonstrate his righteousness, for he himself is fair and just, and he makes sinners right in his sight when they believe in Jesus" (Romans 3:23-26, NLT).

Therefore, "if you confess with your mouth Jesus as Lord and believe in your heart that God raised Him from the dead, you will be saved; for with the heart a person believes, resulting in righteousness, and with the mouth he confesses, resulting in salvation" (Romans 10:9-10, NASB).

Believing in Christ is a soul-deep response. The heart, the seat of the soul, opens to allow Christ to enter and make Him Lord of one's life. When you accept Christ and repent of your sins, Christ births new life into you, bursts into your heart, transforming you from the inside out and breathing into you an eternal, joyful, abundant life. With Christ in your life, you are gifted the Holy Spirit, and your heart is eternally safe in the pure, perfect love of the One who made your heart.

Picture standing in the basket under a huge hot-air balloon. When you accept Christ, He enters your life, and the Holy Spirit seals your body (your basket). God's love dwells within you, and by Christ's love, mercy, and forgiveness, you are saved and rise to a new life in Christ. God's love surrounds you, encircling you, He goes before you, guarding you, while goodness and lovingkindness follow you all the days of your life.

Christ Jesus promises to always be with you, He gives eternal life, and no one will snatch you out of His hand, or our Heavenly Father's hand. Your life is hidden in Christ; your name is written in the Lamb's book of life; therefore, you are signed, sealed, and delivered; you are God's child!

Since you have been made right in God's sight by faith, you have peace with God because of what Jesus Christ our Lord has done for us (Romans 5:1).

"The peace of God is an eternal calm. ... It lies so deeply within the human heart that no external difficulty or disturbance can reach it. And anyone who enters the presence of God becomes a partaker of that undisturbed and undisturbable calm." ~ Arthur Tappan Pierson

Doesn't undisturbable calm sound wonderful, beautiful, and amazing? Knowing Christ as Savior, knowing who He is, His qualities, all that He does, and all the wonderful aspects of who He is, brings undisturbable calm.

Jesus said, "Peace I leave with you; My [own] peace I now give and bequeath to you. Not as the world gives do I give to you. Do not let your hearts be troubled, neither let them be afraid. [Stop allowing yourselves to be agitated and disturbed, and do not permit yourselves to be fearful and intimidated and cowardly and unsettled.]" (John 14:27, AMPC).

Christ gives rest and peace that flows constantly and directly from God's throne. Therefore, "**let the peace of Christ** [the inner calm of one who walks daily with Him] **be the controlling factor in your hearts** [deciding and settling questions that arise]" (Romans 5:1, NCV; Colossians 3:15, AMP, emphasis added).

When we let, *allow*, the peace of Christ to be the controlling factor of our lives, permeating our being with thoughts of God, the words of God, and the praise and thankfulness to God, we find God's presence is fullness of joy, pleasures forever at His right hand (Psalm 16:11).

In Matthew 16, Jesus asked His disciples, Who do you say I am? Peter responded, "You are the Christ, the Son of the living God." Yes, that is who Jesus Christ is, and He is so much more. He is the Lamb of God who takes away the sin of the world (John 1:29). He is the Messiah (Matthew 1:1, 16-18). He is the Savior (Philippians 3:20, 2 Timothy 1:10). He is the sacrifice for our sins (1 John 2:2). Jesus Christ is the door to salvation (John 10:7,9). He came so that we would have life and have it abundantly (John 10:10). He is the Shepherd (John 10:11,14). He gives joy-full joy (John 15:11). He is the way, the truth, and the life (John 14:6). He is the light of the world (John 8:12). He is the hope of glory (Colossians 1:4). He has all the treasures of wisdom and knowledge (Colossians 2:3).

Christ is our advocate (1 John 2:1). He intercedes for us (Romans 8:34). Through our Lord Jesus Christ, we have peace with God (Romans 5:1).

In Christ, we have peace, and even in trouble, we can take courage because Christ has overcome the world (John 16:33).

Christ is the same yesterday, today, and forever (Hebrews 13:8). Jesus Christ is all this and so much more.

Would you be willing to take the above verses and make them personal? *Jesus Christ is the Son of the living God. He is the lamb of God who takes away my sin. He is my Messiah, my Savior, the sacrifice for my sins. He is the door to my salvation, giving me His abundant life. He is my Shepherd; He gives me His full joy. He is the truth, the way, and the life, and His light shines on (and in) my soul. He is the hope of glory, blessing me with all the treasures of His wisdom and knowledge. He is my advocate, interceding before the Father, giving peace with God. In Christ, I have peace, and even in trouble, I can take courage because Christ has overcome the world. Therefore, Christ, and all the wonderful truths of who He is, was with me yesterday, is with me today, and will be with me forever. Praise the Lord for Jesus Christ, my Savior, is all this and so much more.*

And another marvelous truth, Christ, who is Immanuel— God with us—gifts with the wonderful, marvelous gift of salvation and so much more.

His gift has gifts, inside of gifts, inside of gifts. "For out of His fullness [the superabundance of His grace and truth] we have all received grace upon grace [spiritual blessing upon spiritual blessing, favor upon favor, and gift heaped upon gift]" (John 1:16, AMP).

In Christ, we are gifted with deliverance,

redemption, renewal, restoration, and eternal life. We are gifted to be loved by the Father and loved by the Son, a beautiful unity of body, soul, mind, and spirit. God gifts with His agape love so that we can love Him and love others through His love. We are gifted with comfort, for God is compassionate and the God of all comfort.

We are gifted with the Bible, God's word, which is His love letter to us. Every time we read the Bible, God's word pops from the pages for The Word; Jesus Christ lives within us. His word is alive and active and sharper than any two-edged sword, gifting with truth, wisdom, hope, and real-life stories of those who have gone before us, documenting the love that God has for the lost and for those who are His.

In Christ, we are gifted with the Holy Spirit who empowers us with the power of God equipping us for every day of our life. God's gift of His Spirit is more than we can ask or imagine, always to glorify God, point to God, and draw men to Christ's salvation. For, His divine power has given us all things that pertain to life and godliness, through the knowledge of Him who called us by glory and virtue. ... for the gifts and the calling of God are irrevocable. We are gifted with the fruit of the Spirit – love, joy, peace, patience, kindness, goodness, faithfulness, gentleness, and self-control.

And to top off that good news, where the Spirit of

the Lord is, there is freedom. (2 Peter 1:3, NKJV; Romans 11:29, NASB; Galatians 5:22-23, 2 Corinthians 3:17, ESV).

Throughout the Bible, we read of God's Holy Spirit equipping people with skill, craftsmanship, leadership, prophecy, and blessing them in various ways to empower them to do what God had called them to do.

When young David killed the giant Goliath, little David didn't morph into a bigger giant than Goliath; he relied on the immense, unstoppable strength of God.

When Gideon and his 300 men defeated the massive army of Midianites, it wasn't because of their might but because of God's might.

Moses didn't part the Red Sea under his own power but because of God's power.

Samson killed a thousand men with the jawbone of a donkey. That jawbone didn't give him the ability; God's Holy Spirit gave him the ability.

In Acts 1:8, Jesus said, "you will receive power when the Holy Spirit has come upon you." The word "Power" in the original Greek text means the Holy Spirit clothes us with His force of mighty working power and strength, virtue and ability, power for performing miracles, moral power, and excellence of soul, and abundant miraculous power.

Jesus conquered sin and death and is alive and eternal. The same amazing power within Jesus during

His earthly ministry and rose Him from the dead, is given to His followers through the Holy Spirit. No matter how weak our bodies may be, God's life-changing power is given to be faithful, to overcome life's obstacles, to walk in God's ways, and spread the gospel message.

Ephesians 6:10 tells us to be strong in the Lord, drawing strength from **Him**, empowered through our union with Him and in the power of His boundless might. When we do things in our own strength, we accomplish human-sized results. However, when we act with the Holy Spirit's power, God accomplishes God-sized, unlimited, super-natural-results. It's not what we can accomplish for the Lord, but what we allow the Lord to do through us. "Not by might nor by power, but by My Spirit, says the Lord of armies." (Zechariah 4:6, NASB)

Scientists have developed robotic hands, arms, legs, and full mechanical frames to help those with spinal cord injuries to walk. In a much more powerful way, we have the Spirit of God living within us to accomplish what God has called us to accomplish and walk us through whatever we are called to walk through.

We are to "be filled with the Spirit" (Ephesians 5:18).

The definition for the Greek word "filled" means to be permeated, soaked with the Spirit in every area, under the influence of the Spirit, fully controlled by

Him.

The more we love God and surrender to His will and plans, the more freely the Holy Spirit can work God's will and His plans in our lives.

The more we love the Lord with all our heart, soul, mind, and strength, the more our heart, soul, mind, and strength are open to the Holy Spirit and the power of the Spirit.

God is love (1 John 4:8), and God's love has been poured into our hearts through the Holy Spirit who has been given to us (Romans 5:5).

Therefore, since God <u>is</u> love, that means He and His Holy Spirit are patient, kind, not envious or boastful, not arrogant or rude, does not insist on their own way, are not irritable or resentful, does not rejoice at wrongdoings but rejoices with the truth. Bearing all things, believing all things, hoping all things, enduring all things, the love of God and His Holy Spirit will never end (1 Corinthians 13:4-8).

When you think of being filled with the Spirit, rejoice, be open and willing to allow the Holy Spirit to flow in you, revive you, and fill you to the brim.

"Be enthusiastic to serve the Lord, keeping your passion toward him boiling hot! Radiate with the glow of the Holy Spirit and let him fill you with excitement as you serve him.

Radiate with the glow of the Holy Spirit and let him

fill you with excitement as you serve him. Let this hope burst forth within you, releasing a continual joy" (Romans 12:11-12a, TPT).

When I first started dating my husband, I wanted to know everything about him. The more time we spent together, the more information I discovered, the more our friendship grew, and the more my love for him increased. Conversation, fellowship, and discovery, all led to a deeper relationship.

As sweet as human love can be, there is so much more than the love between people. Moses prayed that if he had favor in God's sight, that God would show him God's way, "that I may know You [progressively become more deeply and intimately acquainted with You, perceiving and recognizing and understanding more strongly and clearly] and that I may find favor in Your sight..." (Exodus 33:13, AMPC).

What a wonderful delight to know God, recognizing and understanding Him more strongly and clearly, deeply, and intimately.

"To truly know God as He desires and deserves to be known is not a casual thing, but a lifelong pursuit that ends only when we see Him face-to-face. ... It is simply not enough to know <u>about</u> God. We must know God in increasing levels of intimacy that lift us above all reason and into adoration and praise and worship." ~ A. W. Tozer[4]

Trusting God comes from knowing God. God invites when we seek Him, we will find Him. When we draw near to God, He will draw near to us. Jesus said, "Pay close attention to what you hear. The closer you listen, the more understanding you will be given—and you will receive even more" Mark 4:24 (NLT).

To love God for who He is, not by using our own thoughts or imaginations or what we've been told by others, but to know who God truly is, read the Bible and highlight areas about God's character and love. Discover who God is, why certain things happened, how He worked, discover His heart, and you'll discover the BEST EVER!

For in knowing and believing God, holding fast to His teachings, knowing His love, experiencing His grace for ourselves, and in holding tightly to Him, we find freedom, guidance, and we are given more of His peaceful, loving presence.

"It is a glorious thing to get to know God in a new way in the inner chamber. It is something still greater and more glorious to know God as the all-sufficient One and to wait on His Spirit to open our hearts and minds wide to receive the great things, the new things which

He really longs to bestow on those who wait for Him."
~ A. Murray

The blessings abound in abundance as we learn more about God and spend time with Him and His word.

Who is God? What is His character? God is love, and He is loving. "We have come to know and have believed the love which God has for us. God is love, and the one who remains in love remains in God, and God remains in Him" (1 John 4:16, NASB). "For his unfailing love toward those who fear him is as great as the height of the heavens above the earth. He has removed our sins as far from us as the east is from the west. The Lord is like a father to his children, tender and compassionate to those who fear him" (Psalm 103:11-13, NLT).

God's love holds no record of wrongs; His love is pure and holy, and He sees you through His pure and holy vision. His love is the best, the greatest, the grandest love available.

God wants the best for you, for the best *is* God, and His best is always the best. The Lord is good, His lovingkindness is forever. His love is unfailing, and His mercies are new every morning.

God's lovingkindness, graciousness, mercy, and compassion endure forever (Psalm 136:1).

His light arises in the darkness for the upright; He is gracious and compassionate and righteous (Psalm 112:4).

"The Lord longs to be gracious to you and waits on high to have compassion on you. For the Lord is a God of justice; how blessed are all those who long for Him. ... He will surely be gracious to you at the sound of your cry; when He hears it, He will answer you. ... He, your Teacher will no longer hide Himself, but your eyes will behold your Teacher" (Isaiah 30:18-20, NASB).

God is infinite, and the Infinite is never threatened by the finite. The One who is infinite can fix anything finite "for with God nothing [is or ever] shall be impossible" (Luke 1:37, AMP). "Great is our [majestic and mighty] Lord and abundant in strength; His understanding is inexhaustible [infinite, boundless]" (Psalm 147:5, AMP).

God revives. "This is my comfort and consolation in my affliction: that Your word has revived me and given me life" (Psalm 119:50, AMPC). "I will never forget Your precepts, for by them You have revived me" (Psalm 119:93, NASB).

God comforts. "Blessed be the God and Father of our Lord Jesus Christ, the Father of mercies and God of all comfort" (2 Corinthians 1:3, NKJV). "In the multitude of my [anxious] thoughts within me, Your comforts cheer and delight my soul!" (Psalm 94:19, AMPC).

"Yes, though I walk through the [deep, sunless] valley of the shadow of death, I will fear or dread no evil, for You are with me; Your rod [to protect] and Your staff [to guide], they comfort me" (Psalm 23:4, AMPC).

God will provide all we need according to His riches in Christ Jesus. As we delight in His law, meditating day and night on Him, He gives us the ability to stand firm like a tree planted by the streams of water, yielding fruit in its season, the leaves never withering, and in all things prospering (Psalm 1:2-3).

God shields. For the Lord is a shield about me, my glory, and the One who lifts my head (Psalm 3:3).

God hears and answers. I was crying to the Lord with my voice, and He answered me from His holy mountain (Psalm 3:4). The Lord hears when I call to Him (Psalm 4:3). In the morning, O Lord, He will hear my voice in the morning. I will order my prayer to You and eagerly watch (Psalm 5:3).

God sustains. I lay down and slept, I awoke for the Lord sustains me (Psalm 3:5).

God sets His children apart. Know that the Lord has set apart the godly man for Himself (Psalm 4:3).

God gives gladness. He has put gladness in my heart more than when grain and new wine abound (Psalm 4:7).

God gives a home. He sets the lonely in families (Psalm 68:6). By His abundant lovingkindness, we will enter His house (Psalm 5:7).

"We know that our body—the tent we live in here on earth—will be destroyed. But when that happens, God will have a house for us. It will not be a house made by human hands; instead, it will be a home in heaven that will last forever" (2 Corinthians 5:1, NCV).

God is holy and pure. Therefore, "as He who called you is holy, you also be holy in all your conduct, because it is written, 'Be holy, for I am holy'" (1 Peter 1:15-16, NKJV). That verse is very intimidating. Holiness seems so hard to attain, making me think of a long list of things to do or not do. However, I received a new perspective when I read these quotes...

"Holiness appears to me to have a sweet, calm, pleasant, charming, and serene nature, all of which brings an inexpressible purity, radiance, peacefulness, and overwhelming joy to the soul. In other words, holiness makes the soul like a field or garden of God, with every kind of pleasant fruit and flower, and each one delightful and undisturbed, enjoying a sweet calm and the gentle and refreshing rays of the sun." ~ Jonathan Edwards

"It is a blessed thing to delight in holiness, and surely He who gave us this delight will work in us the still higher joy of possessing and practicing it." ~ Charles Spurgeon

When God tells us to be holy as He is holy, He is inviting us further into the delight of His presence. Joyful, delightful truth is found in God's holiness.

God "chose us in Him before the foundation of the world, that we would be holy and blameless before Him.

In love, He predestined us to adoption as sons and daughters through Jesus Christ to Himself, according to the good pleasure of His will, to the praise of the glory of His grace, with which He favored us in the Beloved. In Him, we have redemption through His blood, the forgiveness of our wrongdoings, according to the riches of His grace which He lavished on us. In all wisdom and insight, He made known to us the mystery of His will, according to His good pleasure which He set forth in Him" (Ephesians 1:4-9, NASB).

We are chosen to be holy and adopted as God's children. **Chosen** -- isn't that wonderful?

In God's good pleasure, in His glorious grace, we are redeemed, forgiven, and lavished with His grace. We are given wisdom and insight to know the good pleasure of His will. God created us for a pleasurable, holy relationship filling the God-shaped hole within each of us with His extravagant love. God invites, beckons, us to be holy.

"I beseech you, do not think little of the grace that you have a holy God who longs to make you holy. Do not think little of the voice of God which calls you to give time to Him in the stillness of the inner chamber, so that He may cause His holiness to rest on you." ~ Andrew Murray

May we pray like the Psalmist, "Pour into me the brightness of your daybreak! Pour into me your rays of revelation-truth! Let them comfort and gently lead me onto the shining path, showing the way into your burning presence, into your many sanctuaries of holiness. Then I will come closer to your very altar until I come before you, the God of my ecstatic joy! I will praise you with the harp that plays in my heart to you, my God, my magnificent God!" (Psalm 43:3-4, TPT).

In 1 Kings 10, we read that the Queen of Sheba was curious about Solomon. She traveled to see him and "test him."

The Queen spoke to Solomon all that was on her heart, asking him hard questions, and he answered everything she asked with great wisdom. When she saw how the Lord had blessed Solomon, it took her breath away.

The Queen told Solomon, "Happy are your men and happy are these your servants, who stand continually before you and hear your wisdom! Blessed be the Lord your God" (1 Kings 10).

When people look at us, are they breathless in wonder as they see all the marvelous things the Lord has done in our lives? Do they see the joy of the Lord on our faces?

"The world is waiting to see Christians live with the joy of Jesus. Once they see it, they will want it. In addition to making our lives vibrant, joy is our most effective means of evangelism." - James Bryan Smith[5]

As Christians, we are Christ's ambassadors (2 Corinthians 5:20). Jesus said His joy would be in us, and our joy would be full (John 15:11). We are to rejoice in the Lord always, delighting and taking pleasure in Him (Philippians 4:4).

Joy isn't only a feeling and emotion. Regardless of what is happening around us or to us, God's gift of joy is here and now, and joy is coming, joy that is promised by God, joy available to everyone who Jesus Christ has saved.

We have joy that we are washed clean by the sacrifice and blood of Jesus.

We have joy for the grace and mercy of Jesus Christ.

We have joy that we are given eternal life.

We have joy that the grave could not hold our Savior, and the grave will not hold us!

We have joy that we are given a new life and a new Spirit.

We have joy that God is our Father and through His son, Jesus Christ we are given a relationship, fellowship, and friendship with our God and Savior.

We have joy that we are the temple of the Lord and the glory of the Lord fills the temple.

We have joy although troubles will come because Jesus has overcome the world.

We have joy because our circumstances never hinder God's joy.

"Oh, what joy there is in the Lord. What joy there is of the Lord. And what strength there is in that joy. God has intended that your life be filled with joy. That's God's will for you. God wants you to have a life full of joy. Peter speaks about the 'joy that is unspeakable or indescribable and full of glory' (I Peter 1:8). Jesus said, 'that your joy may be full' (John 16:24). And He was talking always about this fullness of joy. What a misconception it is of God to think that God wants to lay heavy burdens on all of us, to make us just have to grind through life and barely pull through. 'I just pray God will help me to make it to the bitter end, you know. To endure.' Well, God wants you to enjoy. And the command was to enjoy. The joy of the Lord shall be your strength. And oh, what joy there is in walking with Jesus." ~ Chuck Smith[6]

"There is a joy in the perfect work of Christ, and a joy in our union to him which uplifts us far above all other considerations." ~ Charles Spurgeon

Amy Carmichael wrote, "This morning, Psalm 70:4 spoke to me. 'Let all those that seek Thee rejoice and be glad in Thee.' That's not just a holy aspiration; it's a command. And He who commands enables. Let all those who seek the Lord rejoice, today, every day. Joy is to be the keynote of our lives. He calls us then to make an act of faith every time we would naturally be pulled down into the pit of joylessness, for there is an end set to the sin and sorrow and confusion of the world as well as to our own private trials. We only see today. He whom we worship sees tomorrow."[7]

"Honor and majesty are [found] in His presence; strength and joy are [found] in His sanctuary." For, "The light of the righteous [within him—grows brighter and] rejoices" (1 Chronicles 16:27; Proverbs 13:9, AMP). Therefore, rejoice in the Lord always. I say again, rejoice (Philippians 4:4).

Stormy weather

Can you imagine as soon as we became Christians, we were given a pain-free existence, never got sick, those we love would never die, everyone got along, and we had an easy time and were healthy, wealthy, and wise? Most of us would sign up for that kind of life. Yes, please!

However, how would we know our faith was genuine, and how would anyone else know our faith was genuine?

How could we minister to those in difficulties if we never ourselves had any difficulties? How could we walk alongside someone suffering if we have never suffered?

Jesus warned that following Him would not be easy. James reminds us to consider it all joy when we encounter various trials because the testing of our faith produces endurance, and when we let endurance have its perfect result, we may be perfect and complete, lacking in nothing (James 1:2-4).

Paul said we can rejoice in our sufferings, knowing that suffering produces endurance, and endurance produces character, and character produces hope, and hope does not put us to shame, because God's love has been poured into our hearts through the Holy Spirit who has been given to us (Romans 5:3-5).

The Holy Spirit pours God's love into our souls. His love is poured in *full* so that we can endure whatever trials we face. Even during suffering, if we allow, there are changes within us that flower, grow, and produce beautiful results. Trials and suffering grow our faith, perfect, produce endurance, character, and hope. We can be confident that the One who has overcome the world will help us overcome everything in this world.

During a difficult time in my life, I slept with a loaded gun under my pillow. I needed protection. I also needed strength, so I joined a gym. Friends would hover over me as I lifted weights, encouraging and providing help in case my muscles became too weak to continue lifting. My spotters pushed me to continue the repetitions and press more weight than I thought possible.

I didn't look like a bodybuilder, but my body became lean and strong, and my confidence grew. The more weight lifted, the more resistance given, and the more strength was achieved.

Pain brought gain.

F. B. Meyer wrote, "The irons of sorrow and loss, the burdens carried as a youth, and the soul's struggle against sin all contribute to developing an iron tenacity and strength of purpose, as well as endurance and fortitude. And these traits make up the indispensable foundation and framework of noble character. ... The world is looking for iron leaders, iron armies, iron tendons, and muscles of steel. *But God is looking for iron saints*, and since there is no way to impart iron into His people's moral nature except by letting them suffer, He allows them to suffer. ... Your time is not wasted, for God is simply putting you through His iron regimen. Your iron crown of suffering precedes your golden crown of glory, and iron is entering your soul to make it strong and brave."[8]

In and beyond suffering, God is working in ways we often don't understand or fathom. Yet, divine truths and glorious endings come for those who have been refined by fire and tested in the sorrows of life.

St. Augustine wrote that God had one Son without sin, but He had no son without trial.

In the Bible, we read of those who for their faith in Christ, were persecuted, beaten, lost all their possessions, driven from their homes, fed to lions, sawn in two, burned alive, and suffered in horrible ways. Even today there are those who suffer terribly for their faith in Christ. Being a Christian is not always easy.

Helen Roseveare, a medical doctor/missionary in Africa, had prayed for years for reconciliation and unity between European missionaries and their African colleagues.

In October 1964, after the start of a horrific civil war, she was beaten and brutalized by guerilla soldiers. After that savage night, she was taken with other Europeans to stand before a firing squad. Arguments broke out among the rebel factions, and Helen and the others were taken back to be held under house arrest. A few days later, the Europeans were all taken out and lined up again to be shot. Once again, arguments broke out between the rebel factions, this time because of Helen's bruised and battered face. One of the commanders asked her who did that to her. She replied it was one of his men. In response, he struck her and called her a liar. She replied she was not lying and could even name the man. Furious, the commander said he would call for a "people's court."

That same night the rebels threw Helen into the back of a pickup truck and drove for hours. As dawn broke, they entered a village where the rebels had rounded up men to be part of the people's court. Scared, alone, and hardly able to see out of her badly swollen eyes, Helen tried to answer the rapid-fire questions from the rebels. Then came the moment when the crowd was told to condemn her as a liar.

Helen wrote, "I became conscious of a strange and growing sound – a sound I'd never heard before and probably will never hear again. Several hundred strong farming men broke down and wept. Men crying. Suddenly, instead of seeing me as the hated white foreigner, they saw me as 'their doctor,' one they had learned to love and respect through the past twelve years of service. They swept forward, driving the rebel soldiers out of the way, and took me in their arms and hugged me. 'She's ours. She's ours,' they kept repeating. God had answered four years of prayer in that moment! I had no idea that He might ask me to be part of the process involved in bringing about that restored unity. It was as though God whispered to me, 'Can you accept the suffering now? My purpose is to restore the unity between the national and foreign communities, something for which you have prayed so fervently.'"[9]

"'For My thoughts are not your thoughts, nor are your ways My ways,' declares the Lord. 'For as the heavens are higher than the earth, so are My ways higher than your ways and My thoughts than your thoughts'" (Isaiah 55:8-9, NASB).

Weeks later, two hundred people were attacked by rebel soldiers and herded into two single-family homes. One of the women was expecting a baby and was in great pain.

Being the only available doctor, Helen was

commanded by two armed soldiers to check on the woman. Arriving at the packed house, Helen noted she knew almost everyone there. She had for years been their doctor, caring for their sick, bringing their babies into the world, and operating as needed. Yet, overwhelmed by their situation, not one of them looked at her or gave any signs of recognition.

Helen silently prayed, asking God why she was really there. Then clarity came. The soldiers spoke Lingala, knew a smattering of Swahili, and a few words in French, but no Greek or English. While examining the woman, Helen carried on a conversation in five languages.

She wrote, "phrase by phrase, three languages dealing with a medical examination and later with prescribed treatment, and two languages telling them as simply as I could, in the limited time available, of the Saviour's death on Calvary in their place that they might know the forgiveness of sins."[10]

Then without closing her eyes, she led the captives in a prayer of confession of sin, asking for forgiveness, and that their hearts would be open to receive Christ's salvation. As she left the home, still escorted by the soldiers, everyone looked up with new hope in their eyes. They grasped her hands and thanked her for coming, and she knew, without a doubt, that some had responded to God's grace.

Back at her home that night, she prayed, asking God why the people had not responded in the last twelve years to her gospel preaching. The Lord reminded her, "They know what you suffered that Thursday night six weeks ago. And were not some of them also there at the people's court that Tuesday night? Didn't they see your bruised and swollen eyes, your cut and bloody face? If you hadn't suffered that night in late October ... They would have been tempted to say in their hearts, 'What does she know about it?' But because they know that you suffered then, despite all that they have suffered now in these last twenty-four hours I have been able to open their hearts to respond to My love and to listen to your words."[11]

Helen's suffering, her scars, and her wounds, opened hearts to Christ's love. God took what the enemy meant for evil and used it for good.

Elisabeth Elliott wrote, "If God eliminated the problem, He would have eliminated the particular kind of blessing which it bears."

When suffering comes, when life beats bloody, we can trust that God has a bigger purpose than we can imagine. There is so much more happening than we can see or understand. There are blessings beyond the battle scars.

God's heart, God's unfailing love, is for people to know His Son, Jesus Christ, so they will be saved from hell. People need to know about Christ; they need to know those who have gone through hardships and can identify with their suffering. They need to know the Savior. And your story, your scars, can point to the scars of Christ who suffered, died, and rose again, proving His love for all.

"We are persecuted by others, but God has not forsaken us. We may be knocked down, but not out. We continually share in the death of Jesus in our own bodies so that the resurrection life of Jesus will be revealed through our humanity. We consider living to mean that we are constantly being handed over to death for Jesus' sake so that the life of Jesus will be revealed through our humanity" (2 Corinthians 4:9-11, TPT). "And after you have suffered a little while, the God of all grace [Who imparts all blessing and favor], Who has called you to His [own] eternal glory in Christ Jesus, will Himself complete and make you what you ought to be, establish and ground you securely, and strengthen, and settle you" (1 Peter 5:10, AMPC).

"Some of God's best lessons are His most challenging. When we come to the end of our own strength, we learn to rely on His. Through prayer He takes us by the hand and leads us to fresh places of grace that we never would have seen if the challenges had not come." ~ James Banks[12]

Helen Roseveare also wrote of her time in Africa,

where a school had been established in a village. During an uprising by guerrilla soldiers, a plan was set to protect the school children in case of an attack. Scouts were placed along the road leading to the village, and if the sound of an approaching vehicle was heard, the scout would whistle a sharp alarm. The first to hear the whistle would beat out a warning on drums for the village giving the school approximately four minutes to evacuate the children and hide them in the forest.

Each classroom had a designated monitor to shove the desks around the room as though the school had been abandoned, then gather any schoolwork and lock it away so the rebels would not realize the school was still in use.

Nine-year-old Paul was the person assigned to his class. At the sound of the drums, the teacher exited with the children, and Paul hurriedly gathered the schoolwork from the room. Small for his age, he could not reach charts tacked on the wall. Pushing over a bench, he scrambled on top, gathered everything together, and threw it in a basket.

The sound of the approaching truck was right over the hill, and Paul knew if he didn't hide and lock away the papers, the rebels would see the school was still in use and search for the students. Even though he would be caught, he wanted to protect the others. He ran to the room where the papers were to be hidden and successfully locked them away. Paul then turned to face the soldiers.

Questioning the young boy about any students, the men mercilessly beat and kicked him. "Almost paralyzed with fear, Paul could not answer. He bit his lip to control the rising panic. In his heart, he prayed to God for courage to go through with it, and that he might know what to do or say. Only nine years old – could God help him? He had only come to know the Lord Jesus as his Savior a few months previously."[13]

Paul remembered a boy in his class who was deaf and mute, and Paul pretended to be that boy. At first, the men were furious, thinking he was mocking them and continued beating and screaming at him, trying to find out where the children were.

They dragged Paul to his feet, and the boy was filled with newfound courage as he reminded himself that Jesus loved him so much that He died for him; therefore, for Christ's sake, he could go through anything the men did to him.

The rebels finally decided they were wasting their time with who they thought was a deaf mute, and because of the disarray of the classrooms, the school must no longer be operational. They left Paul beaten and bloody on the floor.

Helen said when they found Paul, he asked if the soldiers had gone and if they had found the other children. When she told him the men had left and all were safe, Paul asked if he had saved them. When she said yes, "There was a moment's pause. Glancing up ... he said simply and very sincerely: 'No, Doctor, it wasn't really me, was it? It was the Lord Jesus in me.'" Helen continued, "faced by the cruelty of the rebel soldiers, Paul had hardly hesitated. God's love for him and in him had dictated the action he had taken; and he was glad. He had found a way to express to God his great love for Him. ... he had peace and joy in his heart: and he knew more wholly than before how much he did love his Saviour. ... God Himself so loved Paul that He had given His only begotten Son to die in his place to redeem him: now they had shared together in a demonstration of that love for others." [14]

Would you, would I, be that brave in the face of terrible danger? Would I be willing to sacrifice myself so that others would be saved? Do I love my Savior enough to be willing to suffer?

Jesus was sinless, He did no wrong, yet He went to the cross in our place. The cross was excruciating, extreme torture devised and reserved for the worst of the worst criminals. Jesus willingly sacrificed Himself in the place of each of us – no matter how terrible our sin.

Christ was punished in our place. He suffered in our place. He took our sins in our place. He was separated from God in our place so that through His sacrificial death, our sins were forgiven, atoned for, so we would no longer be separated from God. Christ took the full punishment for *our* sins so we could have complete forgiveness so that we would be free from sin and free to receive eternal life in Heaven.

The British missionary, David Livingston said that he never made a single sacrifice but felt it was a privilege to serve the Lord.

To be loved so completely by our Savior should help us completely love our Savior. The free-willing sacrifice Christ made to save us should help us be willing to sacrifice whatever God asks of us.

"There are many blessings we will never obtain if we are unwilling to accept and endure suffering. There are certain joys that can come to us only through sorrow. There are revelations of God's divine truth that we will receive only when the lights of earth have been extinguished. And there are harvests that will grow only once the plow has done its work." ~ Lettie Cowman[15]

Blessings lie beyond sufferings. In the Old Testament we read that the Israelites suffered and cried out for deliverance, yet God didn't just rescue them from captivity, as they left they were given the gold and riches of Egypt. Beyond the suffering, beyond the scars, comes great blessings. "In this you greatly rejoice, though now for a little while, if need be, you have been grieved by various trials, that the genuineness of your faith, being much more precious than gold that perishes, though it is tested by fire, may be found to praise, honor, and glory at the revelation of Jesus Christ" (1 Peter 1:6-7, NKJV).

Chapin wrote, "It is from suffering that the strongest souls ever known have emerged; the world's greatest display of character is seen in those who exhibit the scars of sorrow; the martyrs of the ages have worn their coronation robes that have glistened with fire, yet through their tears and sorrow have seen the gates of heaven."[16]

"Suffering is trying and difficult to bear but hiding just below its surface is discipline, knowledge, and limitless possibilities. Each of these not only strengthens and matures us but also equips us to help others." ~ L. B. Cowman[17]

Does suffering bring limitless possibilities? Really? Yes! Trials polish the soul. When we find round, polished stones in nature, we know that didn't just happen. Those stones didn't have an easy life; they were pelted by grains of sand, other rocks, waves, or the steady flow of water; they were agitated, tossed, beaten, and tumbled, yet the process results in beauty.

"Not only are the spiritual things the best things, but many times the spiritual things can be grasped only by letting go and losing out of our hands the earthly things we would love to keep. God loves us too much to grant our prayers for comfort and relief, even when we make them, if he can do it only at spiritual loss to us. He would rather let it be hard for us to live if there is blessing in the hardness, than make it easy for us at the cost of the blessing." ~ J. R. Miller[18]

God is the God of ALL comfort, which means that no matter what has happened, how big or painful the loss, or how terrible the challenge you have faced, God's comfort will encompass you. "Blessed is the God and Father of our Lord Jesus Christ, the Father of mercies and God of all comfort, who comforts us in all our troubles so that we may be able to comfort those experiencing any trouble with the comfort with which we ourselves are comforted by God. For just as the sufferings of Christ overflow toward us, so also our comfort through Christ overflows to you" (2 Corinthians 1:3-5, NET Bible).

God tenderly wraps our wounded hearts so that we can be used to minister to those who have wounded hearts.

Through my own hardships and pain, God brought me closer to Him and a deeper understanding of Who He is. I was molested by a babysitter, assaulted by two guys in high school, chased by a man with a knife in a parking lot, had a shotgun pointed at me as two men tried to run me off the road, and I've been raped by a doctor. I've been drugged and locked up, divorced, stalked, had cancer.

I've had numerous surgeries, hospitalizations, and medical procedures, and over eleven years of chronic illness. Both my mother-in-law and my father faced Alzheimers before they died, and other friends and family members were taken by death. I've made mistakes and had many failures. I've needed to forgive others and forgive myself. I have wounds inside and out, scars from falls, and bumps and bruises of life. Scars from surgeon knives and scars from the self-inflicted attempts to rid the hurt inside. Yet, God used every bit of the suffering. God provided soul healing so that I can point others to God, who heals and restores every deep wound.

Life can be really hard and is filled with minor irritations and massive trials. If we allow, if we submit to the process, the difficulties of life press us deeper into Christ, resulting in transformation as His life is revealed deeper within us.

Difficulties smooth and refine the rough edges and polish our souls. Beauty shines from wounds healed by God, and His light shines forth. Diamonds are formed under incredible pressure, and you too will come out shining through God's refining and point others to the healing, restoring, and transforming light of Christ.

With God, beauty is always found in and beyond trials. And one day, we will be in God's presence, and

He will wipe away every tear, and we will see the grand, wonderful plan He had in place for us all.

"I still believe that a day of understanding will come for each of us, however far away it may be. We will understand as we see the tragedies that today darken and dampen the presence of heaven for us take their proper place in God's great plan—a plan so overwhelming, magnificent, and joyful, we will laugh with wonder and delight." ~ Arthur Christopher Bacon

In Acts 27, we read of howling winds and storm waves lashing a boat on the raging sea. In a desperate attempt not to run aground, sails were let down and cargo thrown overboard. The sailors and the men lost hope; couldn't eat and couldn't fight against the dangerous storm. Yet the Apostle, Paul, stood and told them to take heart, have courage, and that although the ship would be lost, God would save everyone on board.

Paul was only one man, but his actions and reactions affected the other 275 people on board. Paul encouraged his shipmates, and his faith in God rippled out to give strength, courage, and faith that God would save those on the ship.

When one person is full of faith, their faith spills out

and ripples out to others. Our faith in God helps others have faith in God.

In Paul's case, the boat couldn't save them; the sailors couldn't save them; the soldiers on board couldn't save them; Paul's friends couldn't save them; the only One with power to save was, and is, God.

When storms rage and our ship is driven by the wind, even when people make choices that bring negative problems into our lives, when disaster looks imminent, remember God is still in control. He is all-powerful with all power to save, and He is the God of tender, new-every-morning mercies. What often looks like the worst thing can be the best thing.

Because of the storms, Paul had an opportunity to share to all those on board that God is the true God who saves. Paul's calm faith reassured everyone else to have faith. Because of Paul's faith, those on board ate food and gathered their strength. Because of Paul's faith, the centurion kept the soldiers from killing the prisoners. Because of Paul's faith, everyone stayed on the ship until they ran aground.

Know what else is amazing? Those on board had to be shipwrecked to be saved. The boat being torn apart provided objects for those who couldn't swim to survive.

Because of Paul's faith and testimony in God, I wonder how many on board wanted to know the God who saved them, the only true God?

Steven Cole shared, "God could have saved Paul... but let the others perish. But instead, He graciously granted to Paul the lives of all on board. The world never knows the protection that it receives because of the presence and prayers of God's people! Scripture doesn't tell us how many of those on board eventually came to saving faith in Christ, but I think that many did. Whenever you are going through a storm, not only pray that God will deliver you, but also that He will grant you the souls of others with whom you have contact during the storm. He may be taking you through the storm for the very reason that He wants to use you to bring the gospel to others 'on board' with you. The fact that He graciously answers prayer for the salvation of others should encourage us in the storm."[19]

There is a bigger picture than we can see; there is more to discover and learn. During our storm seasons, watch for the God-given lessons. In the storms, we learn who truly is in control—the only One who is forever in control – God.

Actions and reactions cause chain reactions. Negative emotions, actions, and reactions, negatively affect others. Positive emotions, actions, and reactions, bring positivity. And your faith and trust in God will help and encourage others in soul-deep ways.

A. B. Simpson wrote, "may we never forget that the

source of learning to help others must be the experience of victorious suffering. Whining and complaining about our pain never does anyone any good. Paul never carried the gloom of a cemetery around with him, but a chorus of victorious praise. The more difficult his trial, the more he trusted and rejoiced."[20]

Our storms have a greater purpose. "Afflictions are often the dark settings God uses to mount the jewels of His children's gifts, causing them to shine even brighter. ... God trains His soldiers not in tents of ease and luxury but by causing them to endure lengthy marches and difficult service. He makes them wade across streams, swim through rivers, climb mountains, and walk many tiring miles with heavy backpacks." ~ Charles Spurgeon

Storms are merely training sessions.

Every trial and trouble we experience gives us opportunities to discover how God helps us through every trial and experience. Storms stretch our faith muscles to help us grow stronger in our faith. Storms change the atmosphere, cleanse and purify the air, and new life is released as rain waters the earth.

Will we accept suffering from God's hands, knowing there is a greater purpose?

Charles Spurgeon wrote, "your adversity may prove your advantage by offering occasion for the display of divine grace."

God is growing our faith, increasing opportunities

to stretch our faith, and giving us opportunities to share our faith. Therefore, "Dear brothers and sisters, when troubles of any kind come your way, consider it an opportunity for great joy. For you know that when your faith is tested, your endurance has a chance to grow. So let it grow, for when your endurance is fully developed, you will be perfect and complete, needing nothing" (James 1:2-4, NLT).

When storms rage, when life's shipwrecks come, call on God "call on Me in the day of trouble; I will deliver you, and you shall honor and glorify Me" (Psalm 50:15, AMPC).

God responds to His people, and as you respond and call on God, watch as He responds with His divine grace and mercy. Pray, be calm, and let your faith ripple on!

Many trees stand in the back of our property; however, one is my favorite. The tree is very tall and has limbs that reach upward. Even in high winds, the top of the tree sways and bends, yet the base and the roots hold and stay unmoved. I want to be like that tree, growing and always reaching upward and holding firm during the storms of life.

Resting in God during difficult times is tough. I don't know how long suffering will last and how long the bad guys get away with being bad. I know God's in control, but sometimes life is so out of control that it's hard not to just curl into a ball and let life go on around me.

Randy Alcorn wrote, "A study was done in which one group of Israeli soldiers was told they would go on a march but was not told if or when the march would eventually end. Another group was told the length of the march. Both groups were tested for their stress response. Although they marched not one foot further than those in the other group, those who didn't know if or when the march would end registered a much higher level of stress. Why? Because they felt helpless—hopeless—wondering if they would ever be allowed to rest. We do not know exactly when, but as followers of Christ, we do know there is a finish line. We will not run forever. We will rest."[21]

For believers in the Lord Jesus Christ, pain and suffering *will* end, rest is coming, and we will always receive a happy ending in Christ. However, how do we rest in the difficulties of today?

Acts chapter twelve records a time Peter was imprisoned, chained, and guarded by four squads of soldiers. Stuck in a dark, scary prison, Peter didn't know what the next day would hold. He didn't know if he would be tortured, executed, or trapped in prison for years. He didn't know what would happen to his family, friends, or the other disciples. Yet, verse six tells us Peter, chained between two guards, slept soundly in jail.

Peter wasn't just a little asleep; he truly rested and was so sound asleep when an angel came to rescue him, and angelic light filled the cell; Peter didn't even wake up. He kept sleeping until the angel struck him on the side and the chains fell off Peter's hands. Then Peter was still so groggy that the angel had to tell Peter to get up quickly, dress, put on his sandals, wrap his cloak around him and follow the angel.

How did Peter rest that well, secure, fearless, and calm? Rest, soul-rest is found regardless of circumstances, difficulties, or troubles, because true rest is found in Christ. Peter understood this concept first-hand and wrote, "Casting the whole of your care [all your anxieties, all your worries, all your concerns, once and for all] on Him, for He cares for you affectionately and cares about you watchfully" (1 Peter 5:7, AMPC).

Peter rested, knowing God cares for His children, God is always in control, and Peter was eternally secure in the hands of his Savior.

Jesus, our Shepherd, invites, "Come to Me, all who are weary and heavily burdened ... and I will give you rest [refreshing your souls ... for I am gentle and humble in heart, and you will find rest (renewal, blessed quiet) for your souls" (Matthew 11:28-29, AMP).

Shrek, the sheep, was discovered in New Zealand in 2004. To avoid getting a shearing, he hid in caves for six years. The average sheep has about ten pounds of wool when they are sheered; Shrek had sixty pounds when he was found. That sheep thought he was finding freedom, but he had carried a burden he didn't need to carry -- all because he ran from his shepherd.

Please don't run from The Shepherd. Jesus cares. He said, "Truly, truly, I say to you, I am the door of the sheep. ... I am the door; if anyone enters through Me, he will be saved, and will go in and out and find pasture. ... I came that they may have life and have it abundantly (John 10:7-10, NASB 1995).

Go into Christ, and through Christ, you receive a new, abundant life, safe forever in the pasture of His eternal love.

The Lord is my shepherd (Psalm 23:1). "Not *was*, not *may be*, nor *will be*. 'The Lord *is* my shepherd' He *is* on Sunday, on Monday, and through every day of the week. He *is* in January, in December, and every month of the year. ... He *is* during peace or war, and in times of abundance or poverty." ~ J. Hudson Taylor

Rest in Christ, curl up in the arms of our good Shepherd.

L. B. Cowman wrote, "We would be better Christians if we spent more time alone, and we would actually accomplish more if we attempted less and spent more time in isolation and quiet waiting upon God. ... We can never have too many of these open spaces in life—hours set aside when our soul is completely open and accessible to any heavenly thought or influence that God may be pleased to send our way."

Tozer agreed, "What is sending men and women to premature graves with nervous breakdowns and heart failures? It is noise, tension, and pressure. Living in the middle of this world, we cannot escape from it, but we can retire from it sometimes. We can get alone, break the pressures, push away human society patiently, and quietly wait on God. ... You will learn more as you bathe your soul in silence and turn your face up to the light of God. ... Soon you begin to have a sense—it is not an emotion at all. You are as calm as can be, and there is a sense of absolute well-being. A sense of being where God is—a refreshing, healing, delightful sense that can only come from being in tune with God and retiring from crushing society, allowing God to speak to your heart. If I retire frequently to be alone with God, then, when I come back to society, I have something for it."

Jesus invites, "Come aside by yourselves to a deserted place and rest a while" (Mark 6:31, NKJV).

Take a minute. Close your eyes. Picture yourself lying comfortably in the sunshine. The temperature is perfect, just right. Every breath you let out releases your worries; the weight rolls off your shoulders as you cast your burdens on the Lord. Every breath you take in fills you with God's truth and love.

I love the visual from the Message version of Psalm 131:2, "Like a baby content in its mother's arms, my soul is a baby content."

Come aside, rest with the Lord, cast your worries and cares on God's strong shoulders, and float content in His unfailing love.

For, "The soul runs without weariness and walks without fainting when it moves by faith." ~ Charles Spurgeon[22]

Matthew recorded that Jesus fed five thousand men, along with many women and children, then He made His disciples get into a boat to go to the other side while Jesus went on a mountain by Himself to pray (Matthew 14).

The disciples, many of whom were fishermen, who knew how to navigate on water, found themselves in a raging storm. Why would Christ send them out in a boat, knowing they would be caught in the middle of the lake in the middle of a storm?

But then, Jesus came walking on the water.

The disciples were terrified when they saw Jesus, but He said to them, "Take courage; it is I, do not be afraid."

The storm hadn't stopped when Jesus told them not to be afraid. Sometimes following Jesus means being led into a storm. Annie Johnson Flint wrote, "Jesus Christ is not my security against the storms of life, but He is my perfect security in the storms. He has never promised me an easy passage, only a safe landing."

Peter said, "Lord, if it is You, command me to come to You on the water. Jesus said, "Come." Peter stepped out of the boat and walked on the water. Yet, when Peter took his eyes off Jesus, he sank. Jesus graciously reached out and saved Peter, and when they got into the boat, the wind ceased. The storm stopped, the storm of anxiety stopped in the disciples, and their worry changed to worship.

Our Savior doesn't leave us alone in the storms; He comes to His children amid the storms. Storms reveal who He is, revealing His power and might. "And those who were in the boat worshiped Him, saying, 'You are certainly God's Son!'" (Matthew 14:33, NASB).

Jesus came to the disciples in the storm to stop the storm, calm the disciples' fears, and show His power over every storm. Security isn't found in favorable circumstances; eternal security is found in Jesus Christ. We can walk on water, walk through the hard things of life, through the storms, through anything when we keep our eyes on Christ.

Jesus knows the storm you are going through, yet no matter how big the storm, how high the waves, or how the winds lash and buffet, nothing can stop your Savior.

Will we trust God even when the storms rage? In your storm, are you willing to receive Jesus into your boat, into your life? He will always get you to the other side.

Unfortunately, many people push God away during difficulties. I talked to a woman one day and she was in a difficult life storm. During the lengthy conversation, she spoke of the people who had left, the people who didn't call, the people who had let her down, and the people who didn't treat her right. The storm she was facing was real. However, she was so focused on what people did, or didn't do, that she had not invited Jesus into her boat of problems.

We all have been affected by storms, and the world continues to be a constant blustery, violent wind. Yet, just as these disciples experienced, no matter what storm you face, Jesus reassures, *"It is I; do not be afraid."* You never will be alone. Jesus Christ is the answer to every need. Christ is the provider, His power is greater than any storm, and He is the One who calms the soul.

"Remember that Christ, in His gentle sustaining

help, comes near to us all across the sea of sorrow and trouble. A more tender, a more gracious sense of His nearness to us is ever granted to us in the time of our darkness and our grief than is possible to us in the sunny hours of joy. It is always the stormy sea that Christ comes across, to draw near to us; and those who have never experienced the tempest have yet to learn the inmost sweetness of His presence. When it is night, and it is dark, at the hour that is the keystone of night's black arch, Christ comes to us, striding across the stormy waters. ... The storm is not as real as the Christ. The waves will pass, but He abides forever. ... Take Christ on board and let Him stand between you and the tempest." ~ Alexander Maclaren[23]

Turn to Christ, call out to Christ, and receive His presence in the good, the bad, and the downright ugly of your life. Whatever you face, whatever happens in your life, or whatever happens in the world, Christ is rest and peace in the storms, for nothing, no nothing, is impossible for Him.

God has not given us the spirit of fear but power, love, and a sound mind (2 Timothy 1:7). We are given the power of the all-powerful God and His Holy Spirit. We are given love – the perfect love of God that casts out all fear. We are given a sound mind – a mind controlled by Christ in the love and power of Christ. There is no fear in love, for perfect love casts out fear.

"Each of us may be sure that if God sends us over rocky paths, He will provide us with sturdy shoes. He will never send us on any journey without equipping us well." ~ Alexander Maclaren

Remember the story I shared earlier about the young African boy named Paul? When the rebels were nearing the village, Paul had a choice to make. Would he run to save himself or take care of the school supplies to protect those already hiding in the forest?

In that split-second decision, Paul remembered the account of a twelve-year-old girl in Communist China. The girl had been held and questioned for three days for being part of an underground church. Brought out to a people's court, the guards challenged her. "Do you love Jesus?"

To save herself, she contemplated saying no, but in the crowd, she noticed a girl of her own age silently make the sign of a cross.

The little girl held herself erect and proudly answered to the soldiers, "Yes."

She was promptly shot and killed by the guards.

Paul knew if that young girl could stand up for Jesus, even if it meant losing her life, he also could stand firm for his fellow students and teachers. Right then, he chose to put himself in harm's way for others.

We may not face being martyred for our faith, yet every day we have the choice to lay down our lives and follow Christ. We can live for Christ, even die for Christ, knowing our eternity is forever safe with Christ.

Hearing or reading about the courage, healing, kindness, bravery, or sacrifice of others, gives us courage, hope, and strength. We are told to encourage and build one another up (1 Thessalonians 5:11). To encourage one another means to give courage to another. The true-life stories in the Bible, and throughout history, of those who stood firm through persecution, trials, and hardships, gives us courage.

You too can share and tell others what God has done in your life. Please don't ever discount what you do and say.

"The Master's plan – and what a genius plan it is – is this, that the world should be won ... by everyone who knows the story of Jesus *telling someone and* telling not only with his lips earnestly and tactfully, but even more, *telling with his life*." ~ S. D. Gordon[24]

Through sharing our testimony, living lives that honor Christ, others are shown how God forgives, moves, heals, renews, and restores lives. With your lips, with your life, point those held in captivity by the enemy to The One who can forever set them free.

Stand firm. Take courage, give courage, and remember the words of God and our Lord, Jesus Christ ...

"Have not I commanded you? Be strong,

vigorous, and very courageous. Be not afraid, neither be dismayed, for the Lord your God is with you wherever you go." Do not be afraid any longer but go on speaking and do not be silent; for I am with you. (Joshua 1:9, AMPC; Acts 18:9-10).

Jesus asked, **why are you afraid**, you men of little faith? Then He got up and rebuked the winds and the sea, and it became perfectly calm (Matthew 8:26). **Take courage, it is I; do not be afraid** (Matthew 14:27). Get up, and **do not be afraid** (Matthew 17:7). **Do not be afraid** of those who kill the body and after that have no more that they can do (Luke 12:4). **Do not be afraid**, little flock, for your Father has chosen gladly to give you the kingdom (Luke 12:32).

"Behold, God is my salvation, **I will trust and not be afraid**; for the Lord God is my strength and song, and He has become my salvation" (Isaiah 12:2, NASB). "Isaiah 12:2 doesn't say, 'When I am afraid, I will trust'; it says, 'I will trust, and not be afraid.' Faith is not simply medicine to kill the disease; faith is spiritual power to keep us from being infected in the first place. Notice what the prophet puts first: 'Behold, God is my salvation.' If you want to overcome fear, get your eyes off yourself and your feelings, and off the problems that have upset you, and get your eyes on God." Warren Wiersbe[25]

Take a moment and think about the beach. For one person that thought might create a positive feeling. For another, thinking about the beach may create a negative emotion. I love the beauty of a white sand beach and turquoise water; however, I am not a fan of sand that seems to get stuck in any bodily orifice it can find. Even though a beach is a neutral object, our feelings and emotions are based on our thoughts about the beach. A person, place, or thing is neutral. Our thoughts about a person, place, or thing cause our feelings and emotions.

Live by Truth, not be feelings.

"As believers, 'we live by faith, not by sight' – God never wants us to live by our feelings. Our inner self may want to live by feelings, and Satan may want us to, but God wants us to face the fact, not feelings. He wants us to face the facts of Christ and His finished and perfect work for us. And once we face these precious facts and believe them simply because God says they are facts, He will take care of our feelings." ~ Lettie Cowman[26]

Emotions and feelings are ever-changing. However, when we remember the Truth of who we are in Christ, our feelings and emotions come under the protection and authority of Christ.

"If you dwell on your own feelings about things rather than dwelling on the faithfulness, the love, and the mercy of God, then you're likely to have a terrible, horrible, no good, very bad day. Our feelings are very fleeting and ephemeral, aren't they? We can't depend on them for five minutes at a time. But dwelling on the love, faithfulness, and mercy of God is always safe." ~ Elisabeth Elliot

Regardless of how you feel, choose to focus on God, on the divine attributes of His love, and dwell in the peace of His love.

In Acts 28:1, Luke wrote, "after we were brought safely through." The interesting thing is Luke and Paul, and everyone on that ship had just experienced a horrible storm *and shipwreck*. Many people would not say they had been "brought safely through," they would fixate on the terrible time they'd encountered while being in a raging sea for days and days, and the fact that the ship's cargo was lost, and the boat was destroyed.

Paul had years of being mistreated by others. He was beaten, stoned, and jailed, people repeatedly tried to kill him, he lived through several shipwrecks, and he experienced hardships and trials beyond what most people could endure.

Paul didn't sit around feeling sorry for himself, whining and complaining about his numerous difficulties. Paul kept a proper perspective by keeping his focus on Christ. Paul saw each day, and every experience, even his trials, as opportunities to share Christ.

Sharon Jaynes wrote, "History is full of untold stories of men and women who did not complete their assignments from God but stopped too soon in the face of disappointment. Perseverance is fueled by moving beyond the circumstances that are seemingly against you with confidence in the Holy Spirit who is within you."[27]

Paul never sugar-coated the trials he had, but he never stopped. He persevered; he ran the race of life, forgetting what was behind; he continued running, fighting the good fight, and pressed onward. He didn't waste the God-given opportunities he was given. By keeping focused on Christ, Paul continued telling others about Christ. He did at times mention his difficulties, but he kept going, kept talking about the joy of the Lord, and continued always pointing to our Savior.

For a hot-air balloon to rise from the ground, the air inside the envelope must be lighter than the outside air. To achieve this goal, the air inside must be heated.

"To burn brightly our lives must first experience the flame. ... Combat comes before victory. If God has chosen special trials for you to endure, be assured He has kept a very special place in His heart just for you. A badly bruised soul is one who is chosen." ~ L. B. Cowman[28]

If Paul had only paid attention to all the terrible things he went through, he would have missed everything God was doing even through his suffering. Paul looked beyond what happened to his body and the hardships he faced. He never gave up, he had the Holy Spirit within him, and he knew God was always in control.

"It doesn't much matter what happens to us. The one thing that matters is how we meet what happens. Limitations, frustrations—they can't cast the smallest handful of dust on the glory of God. So, let us be of good courage. He is leading us through and on, and as for God, His way is perfect." ~ Amy Carmichael[29]

God promises to get us through our difficulties, but we must be willing to *go on through*. Remember, whatever we went through, means we have <u>already</u> gone through.

I wonder how often we have prayed to be used by the Lord desiring to be used by Him in mighty ways, but then when we are put in difficult situations we think God has deserted us or is mad at us, and then we get angry at God?

Some people have stopped running the race of life because of a negative experience. Difficulties and tragedies can knock the breath out of our lungs and the will to move forward. It's easy to stop, set up a mile marker on the life road and then stay at the marker, grieving forever what was lost.

Life is messy, uncomfortable, and painful. I understand, life *is* hard. Bad things happen and it is difficult to move forward.

God promises, "when you pass through the waters, I will be with you; and through the rivers, they will not overwhelm you. When you walk through fire, you will not be scorched, nor will the flame burn you. For I am the Lord your God, the Holy One of Israel, your Savior" (Isaiah 43:2, AMP).

God is a tender, merciful, compassionate God. He knows life is hard. No matter how horrible life has treated us, He binds the broken-hearted and heals wounds. Our tears are lovingly stored in His bottle (Psalm 56:8). He holds broken hearts close to His heart providing comfort and healing.

Have you ever watched a suspenseful movie? Your heart races and pounds as the hero or heroine goes through trials and difficulties. You weep as they suffer, yet at the ending, when all turns out okay, you breathe a sigh of relief. However, if you watch that same movie again, the suspense is changed because you know the happy ending. God will always bring His children safely through to the most wonderful forever, heavenly ending.

"The next time you're overwhelmed, instead of asking 'How can I get out of this mess?' try asking, 'How can God be glorified in this situation?' One's perspective is entirely changed by the spiritual realities behind that approach. It's like switching on floodlights in a dark stadium." ~ Robert J. Morgan[30]

There is always a bigger picture. There is more to our stories that reach eternal proportions. Nothing is wasted; no pain, no suffering, is wasted. Romans 8:28 is true, for those who love God and are called according to His purpose, all things will work together for good. God works ALL things together for good. ALL things!

"God will let nothing happen to one of His children without supplying the necessary grace to turn the stumbling block into a stepping stone." ~ Selwyn Hughes

Everything God has helped you through can be used by God to grow your faith, trust, and confidence in God. Our trials can be used to help others get through the trials they are facing or will face in the future. God desires all people to be saved and come to the knowledge of the truth (1 Timothy 2:4) and each step of our painful journey can be used to point others to God's saving grace.

Helen Roseveare wrote, "nothing will be allowed to touch my life by accident or coincidence. God is in control, and in fulfillment of His will – on a larger canvas than I can see – everything big or little that comes into my life is part of His purpose. That is utterly amazing! He offers me the privilege of being part of His purpose, part of His plan, moment by moment. So, I can think of everything that comes as a *privilege*! Whether it seems hurtful or joyful, whether I think I can see a point in it or not, *ALL is privilege.* The next step, if that is so, is that I can say – and truly mean – that in everything I *can* rejoice; counting it all joy, even in trials and tribulations." ~ Helen Roseveare[31]

There are greater purposes, greater results, and eternal joy over the horizon. Joni Eareckson Tada wrote, "The best we can hope for in this life is a knothole peek at the shining realities ahead. Yet a glimpse is enough. It's enough to convince our hearts that whatever sufferings and sorrows currently assail us aren't worthy of comparison to that which waits over the horizon."

Therefore, remember, there's more coming, more amazing things coming. Because, "Whatever happens, the worst will only be a weary traveler receiving a joyful and heavenly welcome home." ~ Samuel Rutherford

"With visions of God's eternity and Christ's blessed immortality, we step onward through all the care and sorrow and bitterness and unrest of time by loving, intelligent anticipation of eternity." ~ Joseph Parker

I was raised in a Christian home, went to church every time the church doors opened, was taught the Bible, read the Bible, memorized verses, and was taught to be kind and loving to others. However, I don't remember being taught how to battle.

Christianity is more than quoting scriptural platitudes and putting on a happy face. Jesus warned His followers they would have trouble in this world, be persecuted, hated, and suffer. Christianity is those who walk in the Light, taking on the force of darkness. And the darkness hates the light. Satan is out to steal, kill, and destroy, and we live in enemy territory.

Attacks are going to come. We are in a spiritual battle, and although we do not fight with flesh and blood, flesh and blood can be very, very, **very** nasty.

In a world filled with demonic forces, we need to know how to fight those forces. "For our struggle is not against flesh and blood, but against the rulers, against the powers, against the world forces of this darkness, against the spiritual forces of wickedness in the heavenly places" (Ephesians 6:12, NASB)

To slay dragons, we need to be trained and ready for dragon-slaying. C. S. Lewis wrote, "Since it is so likely that (children) will meet cruel enemies, let them at least have heard of brave knights and heroic courage. Otherwise, you are making their destiny not brighter but darker."

There are horrible things that happen in this world. Evil people are inflicting nightmarish suffering. We need to know how to stand firm when we hear of, or experience for ourselves, something that makes us question if we can survive. Not only how do we survive but how we can continue to tell others about our Savior who eternally saves.

Can we trust God when hell seems to be gaining ground? Can we trust that God is good when everything bad continues to happen?

Dwight Moody wrote, "Those who know most about God trust Him the most. ... Tell the world, tell your feelings, tell your friends – that you are going to trust God, whether you are sick or well; whether you live or die – whatever happens to you, you can and will trust Him."[32]

Throughout the Bible, we are told by God and Jesus not to be afraid, to fear not. God knows we are frail; we are but dust. We may feel like little dust bunnies in a world of Hoover vacuums. Yet, Psalm 103:13-14 reassures, just as a father has compassion on his children, so the Lord has compassion on those who fear Him. For He knows our frame; He is mindful that we are but dust.

We may be dust bunnies, but our compassionate and caring God is BIGGER than anything and anyone, and He will never leave or forsake His children.

During the Israeli 6-Day War in 1967, Yisrael, a cab driver by trade, was called to serve in the army IDF reserve. He, and another reserve soldier, an electrician by trade, were sent to patrol the area around the Tiran Straits. As they made their way, an Egyptian half-track with mounted machine guns on every side stopped in front of them. Yisrael and the other soldier, armed with only light weapons and a few bullets, stood in despair and waited for the Egyptians to shoot. But the shots didn't come.

Cautiously the men approached the vehicle and peered inside. Eighteen armed soldiers sat with guns in hand and a petrified look on their faces as though begging for mercy. Yisrael shouted for them to get their hands up, and the two reserve soldiers took the Egyptians captive. As they marched back to the Israeli camp, Yisrael asked the Egyptian sergeant why they didn't shoot them. The man answered that he didn't know, that his arms froze and his whole body became paralyzed. The only logical answer was that God had helped them.[33]

God reassured Joshua and reassures us in Joshua 1:9 (this is using various translations) -- Have I not commanded you? Be bold, strong, of good courage, brave, vigorous, steadfast, and very courageous! Do not be afraid, do not lose faith, do not lose hope, do not tremble, do not be terrified or dismayed or intimidated, for the Lord your God is with you wherever you go (Joshua 1:9).

God beckons, say to those with fearful hearts; I am with you. I have heard your cry. Don't be dismayed. Don't be discouraged. I will help you. I have redeemed you. I have summoned you by name. I will save you. I am your shield. I love you. Perfect love casts out fear. I will protect you. I am your deliverer. I will go with you. I will fight for you. I will defend you. I will never leave you. I will strengthen you and help you. I will support you with my righteous right hand. I have heard your prayer. Take courage, take heart; I am here!.

God is with His children. God's sovereignty, love, protection, and provision are bigger than any fear, anything and anyone. You never battle alone and are never alone. God is all-powerful. Therefore, "be strong in the Lord and in the strength of His might. Put on the full armor of God, so that you will be able to stand firm against the schemes of the devil. ... take up the full armor of God, so that you will be able to resist in the evil day, and having done everything, to stand firm. Stand firm therefore, having girded your loins with truth, and having put on the breastplate of righteousness, and having shod your feet with the preparation of the gospel of peace; in addition to all, taking up the shield of faith with which you will be able to extinguish all the flaming arrows of the evil one. And take the helmet of salvation, and the sword of the Spirit, which is the word of God. With all prayer and petition pray at all times in the Spirit, and with this in view, be on the alert with all perseverance and petition for all the saints" (Ephesians 6:10-18, NASB).

Draw your spiritual sword and stand on God's promises and remember, "I can do all things through Him who strengthens me" (Philippians 4:13, NASB).

As Christians, the battle will continue to rage until we are home in Heaven. When sinners come to Christ, when God is moving and working, the devil hates to lose anyone to heaven and he hates to lose ground. When God works, Satan pushes back.

The devil wants us out of the way, wants us to run, hide, give up and surrender, and he sure doesn't want Christians telling others about Jesus Christ. So, how do we get through these trying times? How do we fight the good fight of faith and stand firm?

Acts chapter four reports that while Peter and John were speaking about Jesus and that He had risen from the dead, the priests, captain of the temple, and the Sadducees were greatly annoyed, so they arrested the men and put them in prison.

I think it's easy to forget Peter and John were real people with real emotions. This would have been a terrifying situation. Prison in ancient times was a terrible place; there would be no nice, cushy cell with three-square meals a day. The disciples knew what the Jewish rulers were capable of; they knew their cruelty because they had seen their Savior mocked, beaten, and crucified.

How would you have felt? What would you have thought?

I wonder, as Peter and John were locked away, not sure what would happen, did they remember that Jesus had warned His disciples they would be persecuted and face trouble? Jesus had also promised His disciples that the Holy Spirit would teach them what to say when they were brought before rulers and kings (John 16:33 and Luke 12:11-13).

Even when doing Godly things, things that please God, that doesn't mean it's going to be easy. Peter and John spent the night in prison, not knowing if they would survive the night or even the next day. However, the next day they were ready to speak, and were bold and filled with the Holy Spirit. The result? Thousands of people heard and believed.

We don't have to fear or worry about times that may come in our own lives because the Holy Spirit will also equip us to speak. Therefore, preach the word, be ready in season and out of season, and always be prepared to share the hope found in Jesus (2 Timothy 4:2 and 1 Peter 3:15).

Learn, memorize, and saturate yourself in scripture. Stay close to Jesus, stay in His Word, and be ready for any God-given opportunity.

In Acts 4:9, Peter stated, "if we are being examined today." People are watching, examining our actions and reactions. What do people see and say about us? Do they see Jesus?

Peter continued sharing about Jesus. I love what happened next, "when they saw the boldness of Peter and John, perceived they were uneducated, they were astonished and they recognized they had been with Jesus" (Acts 4:13).

Oh, that people would be astonished and marvel at the difference in who we are because we have been with Jesus. Regardless of our education level, Jesus is in us, and with us through His Holy Spirit; shouldn't our lives be different from the rest of the world?

Peter and John were again threatened not to speak of Jesus. But they answered, "Whether it is right in the sight of God to listen to you rather than to God, you must judge, for we cannot but speak of what we have seen and heard" (Acts 4:19-20, ESV).

The men stayed focused on their Savior and refused to be fearful of man. They remained bold and fearless, they followed God, listened to God, and continued to speak what they had seen and heard.

My friend, Cheri, lived in Europe in the 1960s and met a German woman who shared her story.

In Germany during the war, two soldiers had charged in the door where a house church was meeting. Pointing their guns at the people, they told those who were Christians to stay, and those who were not Christians to leave.

Faced with being shot, several people ran out the door. Although death or arrest looked imminent, others stood firm and remained. The soldiers locked the doors, set down their guns, and turned and smiled at those remaining. They then explained they also were Christians and wanted to worship with others who were true to the faith.

The Christian lady also shared she had been convicted by the Lord to deliver Bibles to those living in under communist rule in East Berlin. Although she was an elderly, petite woman, she packed up a giant suitcase full of Bibles. Praying, she dragged her precious cargo to the train station.

A guard motioned for her to stop, and she knew she would be arrested if he searched her belongings.

Instead, he took the suitcase from her. Surprised at the weight, he asked her if she had books inside. She answered "Yes," that she liked to read. Without searching through the case, the unsuspecting soldier carried it on board for her.

The woman made several more deliveries smuggling over 100 Bibles to those inside East Berlin.

Be courageous for Christ. Be bold. Love with Christ's love. Be the person God has called you to be. Don't give up. Keep praying. Cling to God. Grow in Christ. Share the Good News with a world that so needs good news.

"My prayer is that God will raise up men and women who will be so aflame with the fire from the altar that nobody can put out the flame." ~ A. W. Tozer

Following God may mean a lifestyle without permanence while on this earth. Several years ago, my sweet husband had been laid off from his job, and I sensed another move was coming. After more than thirty-plus moves, you can be guaranteed "home" was a topic that came up quite often in my prayers. During that time, I cried, begged, and pleaded with God for a feeling of rest. I so wanted a permanent nest.

During my prayer time, I noticed a little sparrow land in the crepe myrtle tree outside my window. As the little bird perched in the branches, he sang a little song. God's word softly spoke, "Look at the birds of the air; they do not sow or reap or store away in barns, and yet your heavenly Father feeds them. Are you not much more valuable than they?" (Matthew 6:26). That sparrow did not have a nest in that tree, but he was happy "nesting" in the arms of the branches. I realized; that wherever the Lord placed me, I could nest in my Heavenly Father's arms.

God blessed with another reminder. I had argued with God for years about the many moves ripping out my poor little roots and the difficulties of replanting in a new place. When we lived in Texas, my friend, Rita, had given me a gift of a beautiful flowering plant. I had taken and planted it outside my kitchen window. Enjoying the beauty, I shared with God how happy that little plant was since it had been firmly planted in Texas soil.

Gently, lovingly, God reminded me that He is the great gardener. Jesus said, "I am the true grapevine, and my Father is the gardener" (John 15:1). Therefore, if I plant in His vine and have my roots firmly planted in Him, I am always home, and my roots are forever safe and undisturbed. Therefore, "Let your roots grow down into him, and let your lives be built on him. Then your faith will grow strong in the truth you were taught, and you will overflow with thankfulness" (Colossians 2:7, NLT).

As Christians, our permanent dwelling place is in Christ Jesus. Through Him, we are given eternal life, access to the Father, and an eternal home. While on earth, we are just passing through. God beckons, be still (cease striving), and know that I am God (Psalm 46:10). As we come to God, are still in His presence, remembering He is God and everything is (and always will be) under His control; we can rest, find the comfort, guidance, and the help we need.

"A quiet spirit is of priceless value ... Nothing so greatly hinders the work of God's unseen spiritual forces, upon which our success in everything truly depends, as the spirit of unrest and anxiety. There is tremendous power in stillness. ... Instead of continuing our restless striving, we would 'sit down' inwardly before the Lord, allowing the divine forces of His Spirit to silently work." ~ Hannah Whitall Smith[34]

Regardless of where we are, how permanent or temporary our earthly status, we can rest in God's tender care. Isaiah 11:10 describes our Savior, that "His resting place will be glorious." When Christ invites us to come to Him and receive rest (Matthew 11:28), He invites us into His glorious rest.

Therefore, remember ...

You are saved and redeemed by Jesus Christ -- "For by grace you have been saved through faith, and that not of yourselves; it is the gift of God." "for us there is but one God, the Father, who is the source of all things, and we exist for Him; and one Lord, Jesus Christ, by whom are all things [that have been created], and we [believers exist and have life and have been redeemed] through Him (Ephesians 2:8, NKJV; 1 Corinthians 8:6, AMP).

You are a child of God -- "to as many as did receive and welcome Him, He gave the right [the authority, the privilege] to become children of God, that is, to those who believe in (adhere to, trust in, and rely on) His name" (John 1:12, AMP).

He will never leave you or forsake you -- "I will never [under any circumstances] desert you [nor give you up nor leave you without support, nor will I in any degree leave you helpless], nor will I forsake or let you down or relax My hold on you [assuredly not]!" (Hebrews 13:5, AMP).

You are given the strength and armor of God to stand firm against evil -- "... be strong in the Lord and in the strength of His might. Put on the full armor of God, so that you will be able to stand firm against the schemes of the devil" (Ephesians 6:10-11, NASB).

No matter how rough and tough life gets, you will not be alone. -- "Fear not, for I have redeemed you; I have called you by your name; You are Mine. When you pass through the waters, I will be with you; and through the rivers, they shall not overflow you. When you walk through the fire, you shall not be burned, nor shall the flame scorch you. For I am the Lord your God, the Holy One of Israel, your Savior..." (Isaiah 43:1-3, NKJV).

You are not given the spirit of fear; you are given God's power, love, a calm well-balanced mind, discipline, and self-control. -- "For God did not give us a spirit of timidity (of cowardice, of craven and cringing and fawning fear), but [He has given us a spirit] of power and of love and of calm and well-balanced mind and discipline and self-control" (2 Timothy 1:7, AMPC).

Jesus Christ has all authority to give you everything you need. -- "All authority has been given to Me on heaven and earth (Matthew 28:18). As a follower of

Jesus, His authority and power are in us, granting everything needed for life and godliness (2 Peter 1:3).

"So, I kneel humbly in awe before the Father of our Lord Jesus, the Messiah, the perfect Father of every father and child in heaven and on the earth. And I pray that he would unveil within you the unlimited riches of his glory and favor until supernatural strength floods your innermost being with his divine might and explosive power. Then, by constantly using your faith, the life of Christ will be released deep inside you, and **the resting place of his love** will become the very source and root of your life" (Ephesians 3:14-17, TPT, emphasis added).

Downdrafts

In August 2020, three sightseeing hot air balloons, carrying thirty people, crashed. Fortunately, no one died, but several people did need hospitalization. The reports claimed a freak thunderstorm in the area caused a downdraft

Life is filled with unexpected downdrafts. We're flying high and then BAM!, life hits and sends us tumbling to the ground. Unfortunately, many times these disasters come from our own mistakes, our own sin, and our own choices.

Sin can look rather inviting, whispering temptations, promising fun and adventure, and even has the audacity to suggest no one will get hurt. Sin tempts, entices, crouching at doors.

Charley, the Cocker Spaniel, understands. One day the outside door was left open. Tentative and slow, she walked and peered out. A pack of dogs stood on the lawn, wagging and barking an invitation.

Unbeknownst to her owners, Charley ran out the

door, down the front steps, and followed the pack. Her luxurious fur coat ruffled in the warm breeze as she rejoiced in the adventure of new-found freedom.

The dogs ran and played along the road through dirt, mud, and various messy places. But then, the pack kept running and left Charley standing alone with greasy fur and wide-eyed with fear. She knew she was lost, far from her owners, and she didn't know where she was or where to go.

Hours later, Charley was found by her owner. She was welcomed home with loving arms, a stern reminder not to run off again, and blessed with a very thorough bath.

In the early days of history, God warned Cain, "If you do well [believing Me and doing what is acceptable and pleasing to Me], will you not be accepted? And if you do not do well [but ignore My instruction], sin crouches at your door; its desire is for you [to overpower you], but you must master it" (Genesis 4:7, AMP).

The devil wants to overpower you, keep you from God, make you doubt God, and drive a wedge between your relationship with God and His people. Fortunately, you are not left defenseless against the enemy. The next time sin is barking, inviting, tempting, and enticing you to run out the door. Master the sin before the sin masters you, for the One who is living in you is far greater than the one who is in the world (1 John 4:4). When sin calls, "submit to [the authority of] God. Resist the devil [stand firm against him] and he will flee from you" (James 4:7, AMP).

But what if it's too late? What if you've made a terrible mistake? What if sin enticed you and you fell into temptation?

Years ago, we had moved to a new area, and I needed a haircut. Not knowing where to go, I stopped by a little shop I'd seen on the side of a road advertising $10.00 haircuts. Proud of my good luck, I went inside.

Thirty minutes later, I came out with probably the worst haircut of my life. My hair had been chopped, mauled, and the style was similar to someone having their head swirled in a flushing toilet. It was *not* pretty.

Back home, I took a deep breath and stepped inside our apartment. Our teenage son sat on the couch watching television. When he looked up, his mouth gaped open, and his expression was one of sheer horror. As he sat staring at me, someone on the television exclaimed, "You have made a horrible mistake."

Fortunately, my hair did grow back and recover. And not long after that, I saw a barber shop near where I had gone earlier, advertising they fixed $10.00 haircuts.

I wish I could tell you that experience was the worst mistake I'd made, but it wasn't. I've gotten myself in many messes.

Sin often lures with promises of the easy way, tempting with the lines that no one will get hurt and it will be fun. The devil sets the trap, and for those who take his devilish bat, the devil points a slimy condemning finger at the one who fell.

Sweet hubby and I sniffed and walked around the house, trying to find the source of a strange, very unpleasant odor. Although we searched for quite some time, we couldn't find what was causing the nasty smell.

One morning I turned on a light switch and gagged. The odor came directly from behind that spot. Grabbing tools, I took off the switch plate but couldn't see anything, but boy howdy I could smell something.

We tried several methods to access whatever was causing the odiferous fragrance but to no avail. Running an electronic air purifier 24/7 finally did help take care of the problem. Still, it made me rather uncomfortable knowing something might be remaining in the wall.

It's not a good thought, is it? Kind of nauseating, isn't it?

Perhaps sin is hiding behind the walls of your mind, your thoughts, and your soul. Sin always leaves a nauseating stench of consequences.

We've all sinned, every single one of us, and the wages of sin is death. Please don't hesitate to call for help. There is one way to get rid of sin and that is through the mercy, grace, and forgiveness of Jesus Christ.

"When we acknowledge our sin, take complete responsibility for our guilt, and come to the Lord for healing, the poison of evil loses its power to kill." ~ Charles Swindoll

When we repent and ask for forgiveness, our Savior is there with open arms. There is no mess, no sin, no stench, beyond the forgiveness, mercy, grace, new life, and new beginning offered by Jesus Christ. Because of the sacrifice of Christ, we are no longer condemned; we are set free and given eternal life.

The Book of John records an incident when the Pharisees and scribes brought a woman caught in adultery and placed her in front of Jesus. The leaders said, "Teacher, this woman has been caught in the very act of committing adultery. Now in the Law, Moses commanded us to stone such women; what then do You say?' Now they were saying this to test Him, so that they might have grounds for accusing Him. But Jesus stooped down and with His finger wrote on the ground" (John 8:2-6, NASB).

The Jewish leaders knew if Jesus disagreed with the stoning, they would have accused Him of breaking the law of Moses and He would have lost credibility among the people. If Jesus had stoned the woman, they would have accused him of not being merciful and of breaking

Roman law, which did not permit Jews to carry out their own executions, and thus they could have Jesus condemned.

These men were heartless. Joseph Parker wrote, "Their humanity was eaten up by their pompous and zealous bigotry. ... Do we, like the blessed Savior, go forth to seek and save the lost, to lift up the downcast, and turn the wanderer onto the right way? Let us guard against a lifeless and tearless heart that is only interested in exacting judgement."[35]

So, what did Jesus do? He put the test back into the hands of the leaders and made them consider their own sinfulness. "When they persisted in asking Him, He straightened up and said to them, 'He who is without sin among you, let him be the first to throw a stone at her.' And again, He stooped down and wrote on the ground" (John 8:7-8, NASB).

We aren't told what Jesus wrote. Perhaps he wrote the sins of each of those who smugly and piously stood before Him. The men began realizing none of them could have thrown even a tiny pebble. Starting with the oldest men to the youngest, the sound of stones thumped on the temple courtyard pavement as one by one, the men turned and left.

The woman was left standing alone with Jesus. "straightening up, Jesus said to her, 'Woman, where are they? Did no one condemn you?' She said, 'No one,

Lord.' And Jesus said, 'I do not condemn you, either. Go. From now on do not sin any longer'" (John 8:10-11, NASB).

The One without sin pardoned the sinner interceding for her in front of her accusers. Jesus loved the woman enough to tell her to not sin any longer. Jesus never embraced sin, He addressed the sin, told the sinner to sin no more and then gave healing, hope, and a new beginning. No matter how bad or deeply rooted a sin is, Christ's authority and unlimited power can release anyone and set the captive free. What Jesus says, He gives the power to accomplish.

"The good man never ignores the presence of sin. Jesus Christ, with all His gentleness and mercy, did not tell the woman that she was innocent nor did He treat her as an innocent woman. Christ was ever forward to maintain the broad distinction between right and wrong. ... Thank God for such words of hope! The beams of mercy shoot far across the gloom of guilt; the voice of hope falls on the ear of the remotest wanderer! ... The Pharisees would have stoned her, but the divine Savior spread a new page of life before her and told her to begin again." ~ Joseph Parker[36]

Oh, what joy we have in our truth-filled, grace-filled Savior. We have been given new life in Christ and a new page of life for eternity.

Go to Christ for forgiveness and receive His

cleansing. His offer is for you. "There is no form of sinfulness to which you are addicted which Christ cannot remove." ~ Charles Spurgeon

No matter what you have done, the terrible choices you have made, He beckons, "'Come now, and let us reason together,' says the Lord, 'Though your sins are like scarlet, they shall be as white as snow; though they are red like crimson, they shall be as wool'" (Isaiah 1:18, NKJV).

God's offer for forgiveness isn't to be taken lightly. Jesus suffered and went to the cross for our sins. True repentance isn't just being sorry that someone was caught doing wrong, or others disapprove. We all know people who throw over their shoulder a "sorry" for something they did, but the apology isn't true. God knows the heart. True repentance cuts to the heart, breaking open the heart. Repentance is a call to change, a turning away from sin and turning to Jesus who has the power to break the power of sin.

With repentance comes forgiveness, and forgiveness brings restoration and refreshing. God forgives as far as the east is from the west, no longer remembering the sin (Isaiah 44:22). Go to Christ and allow His 24/7 purifying grace to remove your sin. "So repent [change your inner self—your old way of thinking, regret past sins] and return [to God—seek His purpose for your life], so that your sins may be wiped away [blotted out, completely erased], so that times of refreshing may come from the presence of the Lord [restoring you like a cool wind on a hot day]" (Acts 3:19, AMP).

Forgiving ourselves can at times be difficult, but forgiving someone who has hurt us, wronged us, used us, or done something terrible to us, is really, really hard.

Jesus prayed to the Father, "Forgive us for our sins, just as we have forgiven those who sinned against us." Then He said to His followers, "if you forgive others for their sins, your Father in heaven will also forgive you for your sins. But if you don't forgive others, your Father in heaven will not forgive your sins" (Matthew 6:12-15, NCV).

Forgiveness of others isn't just a suggestion but something we must do. Forgive and *you* will be forgiven. What Jesus commands is for *our* forgiveness and *our* freedom.

Many people stumble, trip, and crawl through life because they continue looking back at what happened in their lives, the mistakes, the sins that were done, the terrible thing that happened to them, or what someone did to them, or even their perception of who they are. Driving forward is a real problem if one only looks in the rear-view mirror.

"God's nature is forgiveness (Exod. 34:6-7). If we are

to be His disciples, we must follow His example. If God will forgive our most relentless enemy, we can do nothing less. Jesus did not say that certain offenses are unworthy of our forgiveness. We have no biblical excuse for allowing unforgiveness in our hearts." ~ Henry & Richard Blackaby[37]

Unforgiveness drags down, chaining us to that which we refuse to forgive. Jesus is the key to freedom and has given a key to freedom -- forgive, and you will be forgiven.

When you forgive, the chain that binds you to that person, that situation, is cut. Forgiveness is the ax that cuts **_you_** free. Forgiveness unlocks the chains that chained *you*. When you forgive, the chains that tie you, and the negative thoughts and emotions lose their hold so you can float free. The person remains chained to their sin, and you go free.

You don't have to do this in your own power, when Christ is in you, you have His power within you. Nothing is impossible for Him; He will help you do what He has asked you to do by *His* power. Forgive and be free.

When we come to God for forgiveness, when we forgive others, the past no longer controls or negatively alters our future. "Brothers and sisters, I do not regard myself as having taken hold of it yet; but one thing I do: forgetting what lies behind and reaching forward to

<u>what lies ahead, I press on toward the goal for the prize of the upward call of God in Christ Jesus</u>" (Philippians 3:13-14, NASB, underline added).

Go to God for forgiveness, forgive others, and move forward in your new life. God's great mercy births in you a living hope and new beginning (1 Peter 1:3-4). For, "If anyone is in Christ, he is a new creature; the old things passed away; behold, new things have come" (2 Corinthians 5:17, NASB).

Jesus Christ sits at the right hand of God, interceding for us. Therefore, there is no condemnation for those who are in Christ Jesus. "Who will bring any charge against God's elect (His chosen ones)? It is God who justifies us [declaring us blameless and putting us in a right relationship with Himself]. Who is the one who condemns us? Christ Jesus is the One who died [to pay our penalty], and more than that, who was raised [from the dead], and who is at the right hand of God interceding [with the Father] for us. Now there is no condemnation for those who belong to Christ Jesus. And because you belong to him, the power of the life-giving Spirit has freed you from the power of sin that leads to death" (Romans 8:33-34, AMP; Romans 8:1-2, NLT).

"We can go to Christ through whom we come near to the Father, and through whom the Father comes near to us; and clinging to Him, we can enter into the wondrous fellowship of the Father God, who will draw near to our minds and hearts and wills and make the fleeting days of our earthly existence noble and happy with the blessedness of His felt presence." ~ Alexander Maclaren[38]

Move forward in the freedom of Christ and the newness of Christ.

"The people of the world focus on what they are overcoming. Christians focus on what they are becoming." ~ Henry and Richard Blackaby[39]

For over four hundred years the Israelites were slaves in Egypt. God rescued them by sending plagues on their captors. When God brought out the Israelites, the Egyptian army pursued them. God parted the Red Sea so the Israelites could escape. Once they were safe on shore, God closed the waters and destroyed the entire Egyptian army.

God's rescue had been awesome and miraculous, yet only a short time later the Israelites grumbled and complained to Moses and Aaron that they were going to die in the wilderness and didn't have food. They had quickly forgotten all that God had done for them.

Moses promised God would provide, but also gave

a stern warning, "Your grumblings are not against us but against the Lord" (Exodus 16:8). Yikes! This hit me hard because that very morning I had been worried, fearful, and grumbling about problems in our country and world. Talk about a downdraft!

Why had I so quickly forgotten all the ways God has rescued and provided for me and so many others? Why was I not trusting Him?

"What you do reveals what you believe. If you are living a fearful, anxiety-filled life, you are proving your lack of confidence in God's protection." ~ Henry T. Blackaby and Richard Blackaby[40]

Ouch! Oh, me of little faith.

The Israelites wandered in the desert for forty years because they didn't trust God. Behind every grumble, every fear, every complaint is a lack of trust and confidence in God.

The Israelites grumbled, then God said, "come near before the Lord, for He has heard your grumblings." God is listening. How can I (we) do better?

We are told not to complain, grumble, or argue so that we will prove ourselves to be blameless and innocent, children of God above reproach in the midst of a crooked and perverse generation, among whom we appear as lights in the world (Philippians 2:14).

We are lights for Christ. Any grumbling and complaining takes away our Christian shine, but more than that think how grumbling must hurt the heart of God?

While grumbling, whining, and complaining, drags us down and can hurt our Christian witness, we also need to be careful with our friendships.

Years ago, I was meeting a group of women at one woman's house. During that time, the Lord had opened the door and blessed my online radio show and my writing. One evening, at the appointed time, I drove over to meet the group at the homeowner's home. Sitting in my car, I texted the woman I had arrived. She responded she was still at work and would be there shortly.

Inside the house, I could see the lady's daughter on her computer. I watched as the girl answered her cell phone, then she rose to her feet, and turned off the front porch light, along with all the lights in the house. *Ouch.*

Unfortunately, at that time my desire for friendships kept me sitting in my car until the others arrived. I ignored the obvious rejection by that woman and continued to meet with the group. I kept thinking it was something I did, something I needed to do better, and agonized over the uncomfortable feeling I continued to have when I met with the women. They seemed nice, syrupy sweet at times, and continued to invite me into their group. Months later, one of the women attacked me in a very underhanded and mean-spirited way.

In my desperate search for friendships, I had ignored the red flags given by the Holy Spirit prompting me to move on. Paul wrote, "Now am I trying to win the favor of men, or of God? Do I seek to please men? If I were still seeking popularity with men, I should not be a bond servant of Christ (the Messiah)" (Galatians 1:10, AMPC).

Even though I did cut ties with the women, I continued to have a hard time with that rejection until God showed me a warning Paul gave in Galatians 4:17 -- he said to beware "They make much of you, but for no good purpose. They want to shut you out, that you may make much of them" (ESV). The Holman version reads, they are enthusiastic for you but not for your good, instead, they want to isolate you so you will be enthusiastic about them. The AMPC version, "These ... are zealously trying to dazzle you [paying court to you, making much of you], but their purpose is not honorable or worthy or for any good. What they want to do is to isolate you [from us who oppose them], so that they may win you over to their side and get you to court their favor." Yikes!

There are those who seek friendships to make themselves look better, to give an opportunity to be elevated on social media, in social circles, and even at times in church.

"The important thing to keep in mind is that

whatever keeps me away from God is my enemy... Nothing in this world will in any way feed our passion for God. We must leave the world behind us and pursue on to know God in His arena." ~ A. W. Tozer[41]

People-pleasing is a trap and snare used by the devil in many devious ways. "The fear of man brings a snare, but whoever leans on, trusts in, and puts his confidence in the Lord is safe and set on high" (Proverbs 29:25, AMPC).

Our choice of who we follow leads to consequences. "This is what the Lord says: '<u>Cursed is the man who trusts in mankind</u> and makes flesh his strength, and whose heart turns away from the Lord. For he will be like a bush in the desert, and will not see when prosperity comes, but will live in stony wastes in the wilderness, a land of salt that is not inhabited. <u>Blessed is the man who trusts in the Lord</u>, and whose trust is the Lord. For he will be like a tree planted by the water that extends its roots by a stream, and does not fear when the heat comes; but its leaves will be green, and it will not be anxious in a year of drought, nor cease to yield fruit" Therefore, "Do not put your trust in princes, in human beings, who cannot save. When their spirit departs, they return to the ground; on that very day their plans come to nothing. Blessed are those whose help is the God of Jacob, whose hope is in the Lord their God" (Jeremiah 17:5-8, NASB, underline added; Psalm 146:3-5, NIV).

Time and time again, the Israelites turned from God to worship idols. We might not think we aren't idol-worshipers, however, if our love of our family or friends is more than our love for God, we might have an idol. If our love of possessions (even our comfort) is more than our love of God, we might have an idol. If our past accomplishments, even past failures and difficulties consume our thoughts, we might have an idol.

We may not have statues of idols around our house, but there are probably 30,000 distractions around us every day. We need to be very careful where we focus and how we spend our time. What we think about the most, what we talk about the most, where our thoughts go, where our focus lies, where our money is spent, our strongest attachments and affections -- family, friends, television shows, political parties, social issues, news, celebrities -- whatever consumes us, owns us. What we feed, grows. What we think about can hold and control.

We are warned "do not turn aside from following the Lord but serve the Lord with all your heart. And do not turn aside after empty things that cannot profit or deliver, for they are empty" (1 Samuel 12:20-21, ESV).

How we spend our time, what we watch and read, and who we have as friends, all have an influence on our life. Anything that takes us away from God will leave us empty and deflated.

However, what grows us in God, inflates us to rise on the wings of God.

While completing a Bible study on Paul, I became engrossed in reading what Paul had written, who he was, his relationship with God, and how God used him. During that time, I wrote a letter to a friend with scripture and biblical guidance. When I finished and proofread the letter, I had to laugh since it read like one written by Paul -- *Grace and Peace be with you my friend*. Spending time "with" Paul in scripture; molded my thinking.

If we want to be like Jesus, we study Jesus Christ. Growing in Christ takes soul watering with God's word.

"As we trust in Christ, we become like the Christ whom we trust. ... If your faith has brought the life of Christ into you, see to it that approaching Christ, and appropriating Christ, and adhering to Christ, you become conformed to Christ, and in your daily life, God's grace streaming through you to all, are 'like streams of water in the desert and the shadow of a great rock in a thirsty land' (Isaiah 32:2)." ~ Alexander Maclaren[42]

"Today I have given you the choice between life and death, between blessings and curses. Now I call on heaven and earth to witness the choice you make. Oh, that you would choose life, so that you and your descendants might live! You can make this choice by loving the Lord your God, obeying him, and committing yourself firmly to him. This is the key to your life. And if you love and obey the Lord, you will live long in the land..." (Deuteronomy 30:19-20, NLT).

"Trust in the Lord with all your heart and do not lean on your own understanding. In all your ways acknowledge Him, and He will make your paths straight" (Proverbs 3:5-6, NASB).

> Trusting God = rest.
> Trusting God = freedom.
> Trusting God = Life.
> Trusting God == guidance.

Once inflated the natural default of a hot air balloon is to go up, to rise into the sky. The only way to keep it on the ground is to use ropes or a weight such as sandbags.

Did you realize as a Christian your natural default is to go up? Why? Because according to Ephesians 2:6, God raised us up with Christ and seated us with Him in the heavenly realms with Christ Jesus.

Why is that truth so easily forgotten? Paul asks the same question and then follows with an answer. "You were running the race nobly. Who has interfered in (hindered and stopped you from) heeding and following the Truth? But I say, walk and live [habitually] in the [Holy] Spirit [responsive to and controlled and guided by the Spirit]; then you will certainly not gratify the cravings and desires of the flesh (of human nature without God)" (Galatians 5:7, 16 AMPC).

Don't let anyone, even yourself, hinder you from obeying God's truth and following Christ. Walk in a manner worthy of your calling, walk in love, walk in the light of God's truth. Throw off everything that hinders (any unnecessary weight, encumbrance, impediment, burden, everything that slows you down) and any sin that entangles. And run with patience (steadfastness, endurance, and perseverance) the race marked out for you (Hebrews 12:1).

Early balloonists would often use a grappling hook as a crude landing device. One man tossed his hook out and ripped a chicken coop from its foundation.

Another man hooked a rock, jumped out of the basket, only to have the wind cause the balloon to ascend without him.

Grappling hooks could only provide so much stability. We need to make sure where we anchor. Christ is the solid rock, the cornerstone, our sure and steadfast anchor of our soul.

Therefore, to avoid downdrafts -- get rid of sin,

forgive, and jettison the unforgiveness, stop the grumbling and complaining, follow Jesus and not people, refocus the focus back on Christ, trust in the Lord, throw off any hindrances and walk by the Spirit, and anchor firmly in Christ.

Staying in service

"Whatever you do [whatever your task may be], work from the soul [that is, put in your very best effort], as [something done] for the Lord and not for men, knowing [with all certainty] that it is from the Lord [not from men] that you will receive the inheritance which is your [greatest] reward. It is the Lord Christ whom you [actually] serve" (Colossians 3:23-24, AMP).

Jesus washed His disciple's feet as an example for us to serve others. He said, "whoever would be great among you must be your servant, and whoever would be first among you must be your slave, even as the Son of Man came not to be served but to serve, and to give his life as a ransom for many" (Matthew 20:26-28, ESV).

The original Greek for the word "serve" is to minister and is defined as a servant, attendant, to wait upon, to provide and take care of, distribute the things necessary to sustain life; to take care of the poor and the sick; to attend to anything that may serve another's interests.

"Being a servant of God is different from being a servant of a human master. A servant of a human master works for his master. God, however, works through His servants." ~ Henry and Richard Blackaby, and Claude King.[43]

Whatever task you are given to do, remember "it is God who works in you, both to will and to work for his good pleasure" (Philippians 2:13, ESV). We are servants of the Most High God, serving Christ, called to serve with our every breath and our very life.

Working for the Lord, and serving the Lord, sounds exciting and challenging. However, many people face soul-stretching mundane, boring days, weeks, months, and years with repetitive, mind-numbing jobs, working day and night in thankless occupations. Circumstances may be very unpleasant, yet what God leads us through is often a preparation for us and others.

Moses thought he would lead Israel in his way and his timing, yet God used forty years of Moses tending sheep in the desert. That tedious task prepared him for forty years of leading God's people through the desert to the promised land.

As a little boy, David spent years alone on the hillsides tending and protecting his sheep from bears and lions. And then the Philistine army came against Israel. Goliath, almost twice as tall as most men, stood nine feet, nine inches tall.

The Philistine, confident in his size and strength, taunted the army of Israel (1 Samuel 17). Perhaps the fearful Israelite army desperately prayed for a champion, someone bigger and stronger than the giant who challenged them. Yet, God sent a small shepherd boy named David. And, David boldly came against a giant because God had been with David, pre-training him to be prepared to battle with Goliath and many others.

"When God wanted to deliver His people from Egypt, he didn't send an army—He sent a baby to a Jewish family, and years later, Moses led his people out of bondage. When the nation had sunk into spiritual and political defeat, God sent a boy named Samuel who one day led the nation back into greatness. And when God wanted to deliver mankind from sin, He sent another baby. Jesus Christ came as a baby that He might one day die for us on the cross. God uses small things to accomplish great purposes. ... Never despise the small things, because God can use them to accomplish great things." ~ Warren Wiersbe[44]

The challenges faced, the thankless tasks done behind the scenes, and the seemingly small things no one seems to notice, are never wasted. In the darkness of a cocoon, transformation happens, and new life is birthed.

J. R. Miller shared, "Thousands of years since a leaf

fell on the soft clay and seemed to be lost. But last summer a geologist in his ramblings broke of a piece of rock with his hammer, and there lay the image of the leaf, with every line, and every vein, and all the delicate tracery, preserved in the stone through these centuries. So, the words we speak, and the things we do for Christ today, may seem to be lost, but in the great final revealing the smallest of them will appear, to the glory of Christ and the reward of the doer."[45]

Be faithful in the small things. Be faithful in whatever task the Lord has called you to do. God is in the smallest details, inviting us to work with Him in His BIG picture. The Christian life is not only about us and our own service or ministry; we are to come alongside where God is working. Jesus said to his followers, "There are many people to harvest but only a few workers to help harvest them" (Matthew 9:37, NCV). God invites us to support, encourage, pray for, and work together as harvesters for His Kingdom.

"Jesus did not say to make converts to your way of thinking, but He said to look after His sheep, to see that they get nourished in the knowledge of Him. We consider what we do in the way of Christian work as service, yet Jesus Christ calls service to be what we are to Him, not what we do for Him. Discipleship is based solely on devotion to Jesus Christ not on following after a particular belief or doctrine." ~ Oswald Chambers

Follow Christ, follow His leading, follow His words that are found in the Bible.

Working in service to the Lord is sometimes done on our knees. Throughout history, many of the great revivals can be traced back to the faithful, diligent prayers of one or two people. God often uses the weak, the unlikely and uneducated, the ones no one sees, the ones who have failed and been redeemed in mighty ways. Please don't ever discount your service to the Lord. It's not always what we see as the "big" things. God often uses the quiet ones serving behind the scenes to impact more than ones in the pulpit or stage.

2 Kings 5 records the story of a young Israeli girl who had been taken captive who lived in the household of Naaman, the army commander of Aram. The man was highly regarded by his king, yet Naaman had a skin disease.

Although enslaved as a servant girl to Naaman's wife, the young girl sought the best for him by remarking, "If only my master were with the prophet who is in Samaria! For he would heal him of his leprosy."

Naaman went to Israel and stood outside the prophet Elisha's house.

Elisha didn't come out to greet him, but sent a message, "Go and wash in the Jordan seven times, and your flesh shall be restored to you, and you shall be clean."

The commander was furious, "Indeed, I said to myself, 'He will surely come out to me, and stand and call on the name of the Lord his God, and wave his hand over the place, and heal the leprosy." He also remarked that his country's rivers were better, so why would he wash in the Jordan river?

Fortunately, Naaman's servants convinced him saying, "My father, if the prophet had told you to do something great, would you not have done it? How much more then, when he says to you, 'Wash, and be clean'?"

Naaman did finally wash in the Jordan and his skin was restored. He returned to Elisha and said, "Indeed, now I know that there is no God in all the earth, except in Israel." Naaman returned home a changed man in body and in soul.

If that little girl had been angry, rebellious, and refused to want the best for her captor, she would have missed the blessing of seeing God's healing and her master's salvation.

If Naaman hadn't done as Elisha asked, he would have missed his healing and missed finding that God is the true God.

As I pondered these events, I wondered how often do I tell myself that God will work in a certain way and miss the ways He does work? Even though I may not understand, will I do as God says and leads? Will I be like the little girl seeking the best for those who do wrong against me? Jesus said we are to love our enemies and pray for those who persecute us, and to even do good to those who hate us (Matthew 5:44, Luke 6:27).

"God is looking for a man or woman whose heart will be always set on Him and who will trust Him for all he desires to do. God is eager to work more mightily now than He ever has through any soul. ... The world is waiting yet to see what God can do through a consecrated soul. Not the world alone, but God Himself is waiting for one, who will be more fully devoted to Him than any who have ever lived; who will be willing to be nothing that Christ may be all; who will grasp God's own purposes; and taking His humility and His faith, His love and His power, will, without hindering, continue to let God do exploits. There is no limit to what God can do with a man." - Charles Cowman[46]

Christianity is a life of sacrifice, laying down and emptying ourselves to be filled by God's Holy Spirit. It's not about making our names great but pointing to the greatness of Christ, being open and willing, and obedient.

"When we intersect with the needs of a dying world, we realize our talents, gifts, and passions are not merely ours to enjoy; they are intended as sacrifices." ~ Jeff Goins[47]

As we work for the Lord, one kind word, one hug, one letter, a phone call, an encouraging email, even one smile, can make someone's day and sometimes even save a life. Do all for God and His glory. "To this end also we pray for you always, that our God will count you worthy of your calling and fulfill every desire for goodness and the work of faith with power, so that the name of our Lord Jesus will be glorified in you, and you in Him, according to the grace of our God and the Lord Jesus Christ." (2 Thessalonians 1:11-12, NASB 1995).

I like to plan my day, my life, but Jesus said -- **follow Me**. God initiates, we have a choice to follow. "Jesus sends no one ahead alone. He blazes out every path through the unknown, unbroken forest, and asks us simply to come along after Him." ~ S. D. Gordon[48]

Following Christ is not a straight line; He leads through mountains and valleys, through the crazy, through tragedies, and through the boring and mundane. He has some stay in place, quietly working out of sight of the world, but always in God's sight.

"Therefore, my beloved brothers and sisters, be steadfast, immovable, always excelling in the work of the Lord [always doing your best and doing more than is needed], being continually aware that your labor [even to the point of exhaustion] in the Lord is not futile nor wasted [it is never without purpose]." (1 Corinthians 15:58, AMP).

"O people of God, be great believers! Little faith will bring your souls to heaven, but great faith will bring heaven to your souls." ~ Charles Spurgeon

When our son was young, we signed him up for T-Ball. In spite of the valiant efforts of long-suffering coaches, the skill level of the players was considerably lacking throughout the season. If a "batter" hit the ball off the tee, most of the basemen and outfielders (those who weren't watching the clouds or playing in the dirt) would run to get the ball and then fight over the ball.

The poor "hitter" would be overwhelmed by the screaming parents and coaches shouting at them to "run home." However, telling a child to run home has several connotations and usually resulted in someone having to catch the poor little one before they made their way back to their house.

Besides lots of laughter and the fun entertainment factor of watching the children, not much was accomplished. They needed help to understand the game, and we also need guidance and direction in our lives.

Throughout the Bible, God invites each of us to know Him and know His love, and to come to Him for wisdom, guidance, and direction. "This is what the Lord, who saves you, the Holy One of Israel, says: 'I am the Lord your God, who teaches you to do what is good, who leads you in the way you should go." "I will instruct you and teach you in the way you should go; I will counsel you with my loving eye on you." "He has showed you, O man, what is good. And what does the Lord require of you but to do justly, and to love kindness and mercy, and to humble yourself and walk humbly with your God?" "Call to Me, and I will answer you, and show you great and mighty things, which you do not know" (Isaiah 48:17, NCV; Psalm 32:8, NIV; Micah 6:8, AMPC; Jeremiah 33:3, NKJV).

Years ago, my dad was a church youth minister and approached by a children's home asking him to come as their director. Dad visited the facility, which at that time was only a few broken-down trailers housing several children considered delinquents by the court system.

Dad's first thought was "no." He couldn't see trying to take on that responsibility. He would remain in the church.

However, that night as he slept. He woke to see a little boy at the foot of his bed. The boy looked at him and said, "But, what about me?"

Dad took the position and not long after that, a little boy came to the home that was the spitting image of the boy my dad had seen in his dream. God knew where my dad needed to be and the needs of those children that would lovingly be cared for over the years.

God's plans and purposes are far beyond what we can imagine. He knows where every lost and hurting sheep is, and He will send those who are willing to be used by Him. Be willing and open to God to be used by God.

"All the miraculous attributes of the Godhead are marshaled on the side of even the weakest believer who, in the name of Christ and in simple, childlike trust, yields himself to God and turns to Him for help and guidance." ~ L. B. Cowman[49]

In the book of Acts, Paul and his team spread the good news of Christ, encouraging, and strengthening the early Christians, and God continued increasing the number of believers. Yet as Paul desired and planned to share the gospel in Asia and Bithynia, the Spirit blocked their way.

Following Christ means being willing to be prepared for God's unexpected twists and turns. Paul and his team's desire to share the gospel was great, so why would God block the way? Most of us have probably wondered why would God say "no" when we are desiring to do His will.

When God blocks the way, don't give up or be discouraged. Trust that God has a greater purpose and reason. Trust God, and let Him guide and lead. Trust Him when there is a redirection that God has another plan for you and others. God sees beyond our limited vision, hopes, and dreams. He knows what will happen in the future. God's ways are the best. There are preparations that may need to be made for us and for those we will meet.

Paul didn't sit and sulk or try to force going to those places, he was filled with the Holy Spirit, guided by the Spirit, and sensitive to His leading. Isaiah 30:21 reminds us that our ears will hear a word behind us, saying, "This is the way, walk in it," whenever we turn to the right or when we turn to the left.

Paul's desire to visit several areas had been blocked for now (Acts 16), however, God sent Paul a vision of a man asking for help in Macedonia. Although a man appeared in Paul's vision, God also had women on His heart. When Paul arrived in Philippi, since there wasn't a synagogue, he went outside the city gate to the river where they hoped was a place of prayer. Finding some women there, they spoke with them.

We are told the Lord opened a woman named Lydia's heart to pay attention to what was said by Paul. I love how this is worded. The Greek definition makes it even more wonderful. The word "opened" means to open by dividing or drawing asunder, to open thoroughly what had been closed, to open the eyes and ears, the mind, and the soul.

How grateful I am that Paul didn't just look for men to share about Christ, he watched to see how God was working, and readily shared with the women who had gathered together. And as a result, a woman named Lydia and her household were saved.

We are given other sweet reminders that regardless of our plans, as we stay sensitive to the Holy Spirit's leading, He will guide our way and work in ways we would never have seen if we had not followed Him.

The steps of a good man are ordered by the Lord, and He delights in his way. Though he falls, he shall not be utterly cast down; for the Lord upholds him. A man's mind plans his way [as he journeys through life], but the Lord directs his steps and establishes them. Many plans are in a man's heart but the Lord's decree will prevail. (Psalm 37:23, NKJV; Proverbs 16:9, AMP; Proverbs 19:21).

The older I get, the more I see why God blocked many doors in my life. How grateful I am for His redirection, His protection, and His timing.

Andrew Murray wrote, "I am here, 1) By God's appointment, 2) In His keeping, 3) Under His training, 4) For His time."

"To the child of God, there is no such thing as an accident. He travels an appointed way. ... Accidents may indeed appear to befall him and misfortune stalk his way; but these evils will be so in appearance only and will seem evils only because we cannot read the secret script of God's hidden providence." ~ A. W. Tozer[50]

Trust that God knows the best and His ways are the best. When doors close, remember God knows the plans He has for you; plans for welfare and not for evil, to give you a future and a hope (Jeremiah 29:11). Keep trusting and following Him, and one day we will see the beautiful ways He moved and worked in all of our lives.

Leonard Ravenhill said, "The opportunity of a lifetime must be seized within the lifetime of the opportunity."

Years ago, I turned down an offer to teach a new class at our church. I declined the offer because I didn't know what saying "yes" would mean.

To be honest, and to my shame, I'm not sure I even spent much time in prayer. Instead, I allowed my insecurities to keep me from a God-given opportunity.

I've said no in other ways by hiding behind my computer and keeping my nose in writing. The times I shied away from stepping out in a bold way, I missed time with God, and I missed God's adventure.

Throughout the Bible and throughout history, God's Holy Spirit enabled God's people to speak God's word and accomplish God's deeds.

"All God's giants have been weak men, who did great things for God because they reckoned on His being with them." - Hudson Taylor

Those who believe in Jesus Christ are given God's indwelling, empowering Spirit. Each of us is granted His power to fulfill our role in God's redemptive plan. God will equip you with everything good that you may do His will, working in you that which is pleasing in His sight, through Jesus Christ. (Hebrews 13:21).

Therefore remember, "God has provided supernatural energies for supernatural tasks." ~ A. W. Tozer

We are part of the ongoing journey of changed lives, redeemed lives doing amazing things, and incredible things as Jesus continues moving in His church through the power of His Holy Spirit.

"If I commit myself for the day to the Lord Jesus, then I may rest assured that it is His eternal, almighty power which has taken me under its protection and which will accomplish everything for me." ~ Andrew Murray

An old television show was comprised of a team

given an assignment that seemed unattainable, yet they always succeeded. Did you know that each day you also have an assignment? Anything God asks of us will never be an impossible mission because God is an all-is-possible God. We are able because God is able. God works in us, and through us, to accomplish the works He calls us to accomplish.

Excitement comes when we realize we're on a daily journey with God. God grants His grace, and every favor and earthly blessing in abundance, so that we may always under all circumstances, regardless of the need, have complete sufficiency in everything. And being completely self-sufficient in Him, have an abundance for every good work (2 Corinthians 9:8).

You have a wonderful, divine, God-given purpose. Each day and everything you do can be done for the honor and glory of God. When you awaken each day be aware of everything around you. Where has God placed you? Who has He put in your path?

What has God called you to do, and where has He called you to serve? Oh, how I pray that the eyes of your heart, the very center and core of your being, may be enlightened, flooded with light by the Holy Spirit, so that you will know and cherish the hope, the divine guarantee, the confident expectation, to which God has called you, the riches of His glorious inheritance in the saints (God's people) (Ephesians 1:18, AMP).

For, you are God's workmanship, His own master work, a work of art, created in Christ Jesus, reborn from above—spiritually transformed, renewed, ready to be used, for good works, which God prepared for you beforehand, taking paths which He set, so that you would walk in them, living the good life which He prearranged and made ready for you (Ephesians 2:10, AMP). For I am confident of this very thing, that He who began a good work in you will perfect it until the day of Christ Jesus (Philippians 1:6, NASB).

You are saved by God and called with a holy calling, a life set apart, a life of purpose according to God's own purpose and grace which was granted in Christ Jesus from all eternity (2 Timothy 1:9).

Jesus said that those who believe in Him would do even greater works than He did (John 14:12).

Our creativity and giftings are a blessing from the Creator. Remember, like Paul we can say, "I have strength for all things in Christ Who empowers me. I am ready for anything and equal to anything through Him Who infuses inner strength into me; I am self-sufficient in Christ's sufficiency" (Philippians 4:13, AMP).

The Holy Spirit empowers, energizing as we work by faith, our service and labor motivated by love and unwavering patience of hope (1 Thessalonians 1:3). The King James translates the verse as work of faith, labor of love, and patience of hope. Therefore, be open to whatever God shows you and for whatever the day holds.

As you are empowered and energized by Christ, you will find there is nothing more exciting and fulfilling than walking with God and following Him as He leads.

The Book of Acts written by Luke is weaved together like a beautiful tapestry of God's love, showing the providence of God. God's heavenly footprints guided and lead His people. God's grace called and revealed Himself opening doors for understanding and the doors of hearts to be open to His salvation.

The beautiful blessing of Bible study is as we read, meditate on, and discover the message behind what we are reading, we see God's divine connections and we find the exceedingly abundantly "more than" of God.

Paul wrote, "Now to Him who is able to [carry out His purpose and] do <u>superabundantly more than</u> all that we dare ask or think [infinitely beyond our greatest prayers, hopes, or dreams], according to His power that is at work within us" (Ephesians 3:20, AMP, underline added).

During the writing of the Book of Acts, we read that throughout all of Judea, Galilee, and Samaria, the early church was growing. The early Christians had peace and were being strengthened, living in the reverent fear of the Lord and in the comfort and encouragement of the Holy Spirit. Peter traveled among the believers, following his Savior's commands to go, tell, and make disciples. He followed Jesus while Jesus was on earth, and Peter continued to follow Christ through His Holy Spirit.

God orchestrated divine connections that would stretch Peter's faith and understanding, and do exceedingly abundantly more than he, or any of the people involved, could ask or imagine.

In Acts, chapter nine, Peter arrived in Lydda and came upon a paralyzed man named Aeneas. Peter, so in tune with the Holy Spirit, walking by the Spirit, just as Jesus had told a paralyzed man to be healed and to take up his mat and walk, Peter followed Jesus' example and said, "Aeneas, Jesus Christ heals you; rise and make your bed."

Peter made sure everyone knew the healing was through the power of Jesus Christ. And by telling Aeneas to make his bed, Peter indicated the healing was instantaneous and complete. Aeneas immediately stood up on limbs that should not have been able to stand.

God cares for the suffering and cares for the lost. Some of you are waiting for healing and are praying for healing for yourself or a loved one. Sometimes healing comes here on earth, and sometimes it comes as we, or our loved ones, step into our loving Savior's arms. Please know, that God cares, but there is always more God is doing behind the scenes.

Aeneas had been bedridden for eight years. That is a long wait, but behind his healing was a much bigger picture. God always does superabundantly more than we could ask or imagine, and Aeneas became a visual testimony of the power and healing of Jesus Christ. What happened was more than one man's physical healing; the "more than" of God led to all who saw Aeneas in the towns of Lydda and Sharon turning to Christ. There's always more than we can see.

Next, Peter was summoned to Joppa by two men who asked him to not delay in coming. Dorcas (Tabitha), a disciple, a woman known by her faith, kindness, and abounding good works, had become ill and died. Her friends mourned her loss, washed her body, and laid her in an upper room. Washing the body was common for those in the Jewish faith, but usually, burial was done within twenty-four hours. One commentator noted that what Tabitha's friends had done, didn't seem like they were preparing her body for burial, but for resurrection.

There had been no mention of the men telling Peter that Tabitha was already dead. Even though the Lord had granted Peter great power to heal and do signs and wonders, this was probably not what he expected.

As I thought about Peter standing over Tabitha's body with all the women crying and showing him all the good works Tabitha had done, Peter knew he had no power in himself for so great a task. In the midst of all the sorrow and pain around him, perhaps Peter was confident in what would happen next, or I wonder if he felt like he did when he was about to step out of the boat in the middle of a storm and walk on water with Jesus?

We don't know what Peter was thinking, but we do know he put them all out of the room, knelt down, and prayed.

When the unexpected comes, when our faith is being stretched, for anything and everything, always, for all reasons, stay in prayer.

Peter prayed to the One who has all power over life and death. He took the leap of faith, putting his trust in our all-is-possible God. Peter had witnessed Jesus raise people from the dead. He had heard Jesus in Mark 5:41, tell Darius' daughter "Little girl, I say to you, arise." So, Peter, as his Savior had done, turned to the body, and said "Tabitha, arise."

The woman opened her eyes, and when she saw Peter, she sat up. He gave her his hand and raised her up. Then, calling the people he presented Tabitha alive. The resurrection became known throughout all Joppa, and many believed in the Lord. The "more than" of God was one woman brought back to earthly life, and MANY received eternal life.

I love that Luke included this story. The text highlights God's continued tender care of widows and those who are suffering. It's also clear that Tabitha did not get sick and die because of sinful actions -- even good people full of good works and charity get sick and die. Tabitha's death was a divine set up to show the ongoing divine, resurrecting power of Jesus Christ.

We don't have any record of Tabitha's words, but her works imprinted and revived the hearts of all she touched. Please don't ever downplay any service you do for others in the name of the Lord.

Luke then mentioned that Peter stayed with Simon the Tanner. This is also an interesting note. Tanners, people who worked with dead animals, were considered unclean by the Jews. A tanner's house would definitely be a stinky place. Peter was continuing to progress in his view of God's grace and acceptance. And, Peter's understanding was about to get an even bigger readjustment, and a man named Cornelius was about to get an understanding beyond what he could imagine.

Cornelius, a Roman centurion in Caesarea, was described as a devout man who feared God with all his household, gave alms generously to the people, and prayed continually to God (Acts 10). The majority of

Romans had many gods, but Cornelius feared God, drew near to God, and God was going to draw near to him.

God sees those who are seeking Him, and God in His amazing grace and mercy, reached out. Cornelius as a Gentile was considered unclean by the Jew. Yet, God knew his name, his heart, and deeds, and at about 3:00 in the afternoon, Cornelius saw clearly in a vision (which is sight divinely granted) an angel of God.

An angel came in and called him by name. Cornelius stared in terror. For a centurion to be terrified, tells us just some of the reality of how angels must appear. Angels are not little powerless chubby babies with wings or sweet-looking women in dresses. God's angels are powerful messengers and warriors of God.

The angel told Cornelius his prayers and contributions had risen to God, then told him to send men to Joppa and bring one Simon who is called Peter who was lodging with one Simon, a tanner, whose house is by the sea. I love how clear and precise the command and directions are for Cornelius.

No matter where someone is, no matter where they are going, regardless of their spiritual state or physical address, no matter how lost someone is, God knows right where they are.

Once the angel departed, Cornelius immediately acted based on the orders given to him. He called two of his servants and a devout soldier and told them everything that happened and sent them to Joppa. Cornelius didn't know what to expect, but his obedience was about to bring amazing grace-filled blessings.

We may not see what is ahead, but every step forward in obedience to God leads to the blessings of God opening more doors, opening more of our understanding, and the excitement of seeing more of what God is doing and how He is working.

Brother Andrew wrote, "That's the excitement in obedience – finding out later what God had in mind."

The next day as the men were approaching Joppa, God was again at work. Peter went up to the roof to pray, became hungry, wanted something to eat, fell into a trance, and saw the heavens open and something like a great sheet descending. In the sheet were all kinds of animals and reptiles and birds of the air.

A voice said, "Rise, Peter; kill and eat." But Peter refused, "By no means, Lord; for I have never eaten anything that is common or unclean." The voice came to him again a second time, "What God has made clean, do not call common." This happened three times.

Peter was hungry for food, but God wanted him hungry for God's truth, to see from God's perspective to reach the lost (regardless of their heritage). God continued to help Peter step further out of the box of his own understanding.

In God's perfect timing, while Peter remained curious as to what the three visions meant, the men sent by Cornelius stood at the gate calling for Peter. The Spirit told Peter that three men were looking for him and to rise, go down, and accompany them without hesitation, for God had sent them.

Peter invited the men to stay which is a BIG out-of-the-box thing. Jewish men did not invite Gentile men into homes. Yet, Peter was open and teachable to what God was doing, to follow God's leading, and to be obedient even when it was way out of the box of his comfort zone.

On the following day, they entered Caesarea, even though there was no humanly way Cornelius could have known when they would arrive, he expected big things from God and had gathered together many people including his relatives and close friends.

Peter entered Cornelius' house which is another BIG thing. Jewish people did not associate with Gentiles. However, Peter was obedient to God and continued to step out in faith to follow God. Peter told them "God has shown me that I should not call any person common or unclean. So, when I was sent for, I came without objection." Peter had connected the visual from God.

Cornelius told Peter about his angelic visitor and the directions he had been given to send for him, and that they were gathered together in the presence of God to hear all that he had been commanded by the Lord. Cornelius' heart is so ready to receive -- talk about teachable!

I love the statement that they were in the presence of God, waiting to hear from God. Oh, that we would understand and remember we too are in the presence of God and that we would be prepared and ready to hear what God wants to share with us.

Peter said, "Truly I understand that God shows no partiality, but in every nation, anyone who fears him and does what is right is acceptable to him. As for the word that he sent to Israel, preaching good news of peace through Jesus Christ (He is Lord of all)."

Peter had seen God heal Aeneas and bring Tabitha back to life, but what seemed to be the biggest impact on Peter was finally understanding that salvation is truly a blessing for all who will receive Christ as Lord.

In Revelation, we are told that in heaven there will be people from "every nation, from all tribes and peoples and languages." There is no partiality with God. There is no prejudice with God. **The good news is for all!** Can we as brothers and sisters-in-Christ, from various places, races, and different backgrounds, stop and say hallelujah and Praise God!

Peter continued, "you yourselves know what happened...how God anointed Jesus of Nazareth with the Holy Spirit and with power. He went about doing good and healing all who were oppressed by the devil, for God was with him."

I love that what God had done through Jesus was widely known. Think of the impact Jesus made! Good news travels fast! Now, Peter was going to share the rest of the story, the even BETTER GOOD NEWS! Peter told them how he and others were witnesses to all Jesus did. That Jesus was put to death on a cross but God raised him on the third day, and then Christ appeared to them eating and drinking after His resurrection. And that He had commanded them to preach and to testify that Jesus Christ is the one appointed by God to be judge of the living and the dead. And that all the prophets bore witness that everyone who believes in Him receives forgiveness of sins through His name.

While Peter was still speaking the Holy Spirit fell on all who heard the word. The new believers, just as on the day of Pentecost, began speaking in tongues and glorifying God. Then Peter said, "Can anyone withhold water for baptizing these people, who have received the Holy Spirit just as we have?" And he commanded them to be baptized in the name of Jesus Christ.

The Holy Spirit connected the dots for Peter, and the Holy Spirit connected the Gentiles to believe. God opened the understanding of His people and opened the understanding so others could become His people.

Meanwhile, back in Jerusalem, the other believers heard the Gentiles had received the word of God. When Peter returned to Jerusalem, they weren't rejoicing but critical of Peter for being with, and eating with, uncircumcised men. Peter didn't argue, he stated facts. Stated what happened to him – the vision God had given him, the words God had spoken to him, the journey he took and what he found, what had happened, what God did, and how God moved.

Then they fell silent. What happened was not what they expected, not what they understood would happen, but they took time to be still, they stopped and processed, remembering that God is God. They listened and saw what the Lord had done.

The Jerusalem brothers took time to be silent and process, and then they got it! They had a teachable spirit, and the divine dots connected, and they glorified God.

Let's look at the connected dots of the "more than" of God.

Cornelius receives an angelic visitor. →

Obeys and calls for Peter. →

Peter receives a vision. →

Peter obeys God and goes with men. →

Peter understands God's plan for salvation is open to all who will receive. →

Peter shares the gospel message. →

Salvation comes to the Gentiles. →
The Spirit falls on the Gentiles. →
Jerusalem brothers understand and glorify God. →
The Gospel continues to spread. → → → → God's ripple effects, continue to ripple throughout the ages as the gospel continues to spread.

Let's glorify God for who He is and the incredible "more than" of His amazing, wonderful grace through His Son, Jesus Christ.

Be faithful in service to our Lord watching for God's "more than." Stay in prayer, don't lean on your own understanding, obey God knowing that obedience leads to blessings. Be ready, faithful, teachable, open to God, and share the Good News!

Powered up

In Acts 16, while Paul and Silas were going to a place of prayer, a demon-possessed girl started following them and shouting.

How many times have you been interrupted when you are trying to pray?

Andrew Murray wrote, "In the conflict between Satan and the believer, God's child can conquer everything by prayer. Is it any wonder that Satan does his utmost to snatch that weapon from the Christian, or to hinder him in the use of it?"

There is power in prayer, power as we connect our soul with the One who made our soul. Prayer brings power to overcome, brings comfort, wisdom, and guidance. Prayer is our offensive weapon against the enemy. No wonder Satan hates when we go to God in prayer.

The demon-possessed girl followed Paul and Silas crying out, "These men are servants of the Most High God, who proclaim to you the way of salvation."

When reading her statement, it doesn't sound so bad. She's telling who they are and what they are doing. Wouldn't that be a positive? Nope. The original Greek translation tells us that her crying out meant she was "croaking" (as a raven), screaming, or shrieking. She would have been a horrible distraction to Paul and to everyone around.

Fortunately, Paul knew the power of Christ and knew he had the power of Christ within him. When Paul finally had enough, he commanded the demon to come out of her.

I wonder what would happen if we truly understood the power we are given through the power of Christ and our all-powerful God? No matter how young or old we are, or the weakness of our bodies, we have the immeasurable greatness of God's power, strengthened with all power, according to the working of His great and glorious might (Ephesians 1:19, Colossians 1:11). Therefore, be strong in the Lord and in the strength of His might. Put on the full armor of God, so that you will be able to stand firm against the schemes of the devil (Ephesians 6:10-11).

After the demon was driven out of the girl, and her owners saw their profit gone, they seized Paul and Silas. The men were beaten with rods, thrown in an inner prison, and their feet fastened in stocks.

Even though these men were treated unjustly and

suffered terribly, Luke reported, "About midnight Paul and Silas were praying and singing hymns to God, and the prisoners were listening to them."

Most likely the men were singing scripture, perhaps from the Psalms. I wonder would they have been singing and praying Psalm 121? "I lift up my eyes to the hills. From where does my help come? My help comes from the Lord, who made heaven and earth. He will not let your foot be moved; he who keeps you will not slumber. Behold, he who keeps Israel will neither slumber nor sleep. The Lord is your keeper; the Lord is your shade on your right hand. The sun shall not strike you by day, nor the moon by night. The Lord will keep you from all evil; he will keep your life. The Lord will keep your going out and your coming in from this time forth and forevermore" (Psalm 121).

While they were singing and praying, God's power fell. Suddenly there was a great earthquake so that the foundations of the prison were shaken and all the cell doors were opened, and everyone's chains were unfastened.

Paul and Silas knew something many people do not understand. They were prepared for life's difficulties and enemy attacks by remembering the power of prayer and praise. Prayer and praise shakes things up, shakes foundations, and sets prisoners free.

When we praise and pray, it frees us and there is

also a mighty domino effect causing a chain reaction to break the chains of others. There is GREAT power in prayer and praise beyond what we can imagine or conceive.

Prayer "surmounts or removes all obstacles, overcomes every resisting force, and gains its ends in the face of invincible hindrances." ~ E.M. Bounds

When we pray, when we sing and pray scripture, it releases God's power and feeds our souls. Praising God lifts our eyes off our problems and up to our all-powerful, eternal-loving God. Singing scripture, and praying scripture, gives power, for there is power in the word of God. God's word never returns void. His word is truth and life.

The devil tries to convince us that praying and praising God during a difficult time doesn't make sense. Yet, Wesley Duewel reminds us that "Praise pierces the darkness, dynamites long standing obstructions, and sends the demons of hell fleeing. ... Praise is the Christian's heavy artillery; praise is more effective in spiritual warfare than is an atom bomb in military battle."[51]

Don't ever forget the mighty, amazing power of prayer and praise. When you are in a battle, pray and praise. For, praise defeats the enemy. 2 Chronicles 20:22 reports the time the Israelites were going into battle and sent the praise and worship team out front.

When they began to sing and praise, the Lord set an ambush against and routed the enemy.

Praise God for He is bigger than all our problems. He is bigger than anything and anyone we face. No matter how your voice sounds, whether you can carry a tune or not, there is power in singing hymns and speaking and praising using God's word. Quote scripture out loud, sing praises out loud and use your voice to speak words of life and truth.

There are videos that show the effect of tone on substances such as salt. Salt was placed on a metallic plate and sound waves were played. Positive spoken words, music, and tones formed beautiful geometric shapes. Negative tones created irregular shapes of disharmony and disunity.

Proverbs 18:21 tells us that death and life are in the power of the tongue. Can you imagine the life-giving power of God's beautiful word on the substance of our being (and those around us) as we praise and pray?

When Paul and Silas prayed and sang hymns, God moved. Chains fell off, prison doors were opened, and yet the prisoners remained in their cells. God put a holy hush, a holy pause on the prisoners because God had more planned than a jail escape. Because of what happened, the jailer and each of those in his household accepted Christ as their Savior.

Can you imagine the joy as each person came to the

realization that Jesus Christ died for their sins and they had a merciful, forgiving Savior?

When we praise, when we are thankful to God, praise and thanksgiving invites us into God's courts, and in God's presence, we find the fullness of joy (Psalm 100:4 and Psalm 16:11). Therefore, "Let us come before His presence with thanksgiving; let us shout joyfully to Him with psalms" (Psalm 95:2, NKJV).

Praise and thankfulness, gratitude to God, lifts our eyes, our thoughts and our minds, to adjust how we view life, and how we view our situations and circumstances, helping us rise above and rest in God.

"The very act of prayer is a blessing. To pray is, as it were, to bathe in a cool, swirling stream and so to escape the heat of earth's summer sun. To pray is to mount on eagle's wings above the clouds and get into the clear heaven where God dwells. To pray is to enter the treasure-house of God and to gather riches out of an inexhaustible storehouse. To pray is to grasp heaven in one's arms, to embrace the Deity within one's soul, and to feel one's body made a temple of the Holy Spirit." ~ Charles Spurgeon[52]

Oh, what joy is found in prayer. Prayer is an invitation to commune with The One who created you, who loves you with an unfailing love, and who desired so much to fellowship with you that His Son died for you.

Prayer is a divine blessing to commune with The Divine. Prayer is resting in the tender arms of the One who holds you close to His heart.

We often don't know how to word our prayers, but the Holy Spirit helps us in our weakness, interceding on our behalf according to God's will (Romans 8:26-27). And Jesus Christ, our Savior, stands at the right hand of God also interceding for us (Romans 8:34).

How sweet to know when we don't have the words, when we don't even know how to pray, or can't do anything but cry and groan, the Holy Spirit and Christ will take what little we offer and translate on my behalf to God.

"So, we can simply pour from the fullness of our heart the burden of our spirit and the sorrow that seems to crush us. We can know that He hears, loves, understands, receives, and separates from our prayer everything that is in error, imperfect, or wrong. And then he presents the remainder, along with the incense of the great High Priest, before His throne on high. We may be assured that our prayer is heard, accepted, and answered in His name." ~ A. B. Simpson[53]

"The holy and most glorious God invites us to come to Him to converse with Him, to ask from Him such things as we need, and to experience what a blessing there is in fellowship with Him. He has created us in His own image and has redeemed us by His own Son, so that in prayer with Him we might find our highest glory and salvation." ~ Andrew Murray

In Acts 12, we read that "Peter was kept in prison, but earnest prayer for him was made to God by the church" (Acts 12:5). Peter was guarded by four squads of soldiers. I wonder if Peter was able to convert any of those soldiers guarding him? Either way, I bet they heard the gospel message.

Peter was bound in chains, stuck in prison, yet the early believers had something mightier than Herod, four squads of soldiers, and prison cells -- they had prayer.

Prayer is powerful and has an amazing bonus blessing when we pray together. Jesus said in Matthew 18:20 that where two or three are gathered in His name, He is among them. What a sweet blessing and gift we are given as we gather together, the Lord is with us.

James 5:16 Amplified version reminds, "The earnest (heartfelt, continued) prayer of a righteous man makes tremendous power available [dynamic in its working]." The King James Version reads "The effectual fervent prayer of a righteous man availeth much." The Greek definition for praying in that manner means to put forth power, to be hot, to boil, to glow, to be strong, to have power as shown by extraordinary deeds, to exert, wield power, to have strength to overcome, and to be a force.

Throughout the Bible and throughout history, prayers have routed enemies, set prisoners free, changed lives, saved lives, and altered the destiny of nations. Mustard seed sized-faith moves mountains, so can you imagine what our earnest, faith-filled prayers could accomplish?

"Prayer is the mechanism that brings down the power of heaven into your experience. It is the divinely authorized method that activates your spiritual armor and makes it effective. Prayer alerts the enemy to your awareness of his intentions while safeguarding you from his attacks. It is his kryptonite. It is what weakens and unravels all his ploys against you." ~ Priscilla Shirer[54]

I love this quote by Annie Dillard, "Does anyone have the foggiest idea what sort of power we so blindly invoke? Or, as I suspect, does not one believe a word of it? The churches are children, playing on the floor with their chemistry sets, mixing up a batch of TNT to kill a Sunday morning. ... It is madness to wear ladies' straw hats and velvet hats to church; we should all be wearing crash helmets. Ushers should issue life preservers and signal flares; they should lash us to our pews."

Yes, and amen! Are we expecting big things from our BIG God? May we humbly bow before our all-mighty God and pray earnestly with soul-deep and passionate prayers remembering nothing is impossible for God.

There are Christians living in countries undergoing horrible persecution. Many of these people have incredible faith and witness many miracles. They expect God to work in mighty ways and therefore see Him work in mighty ways.

Our world is a mess. Friends, relatives, and many are chained by addictions, chained by circumstances, chained in the dark by the lies of the enemy, and in need of physical, spiritual, or mental healing. They may be locked in sin, trapped in what seems impossible odds, but nothing is too big for our God.

With Jesus living within us, we have HIS power. Our prayers are powerful because our God is ALL-POWERFUL, so keep praying!

"Prayer isn't a puddle on the sidewalk of life that we tiptoe through. It's an ocean that thrashes us in its fury. It's not a splash, but a tidal wave. We speak of falling in love, to convey the feeling of being swept away by something greater than ourselves. There's a 'falling in prayer' too, where real prayer demands more than we expect. It's often more intense and more life changing than we anticipate ... We get so little out of our prayers because we bring so little into them. If you're hungry for more in your relationship with God, make a point of expressing every bit of that hunger in your prayers." Dr. Rob Currie[55]

Back to Peter in prison. An angel rescued Peter (who had been sleeping so soundly he thought it all was a dream). His chains fell off and the prison cell doors opened. I wondered why the many guards didn't notice as Peter was released passing through two gates inside the prison and the gate leading to the city? I thought of the verse in John 1:5, that a light shines in the darkness, and the darkness could not overcome or comprehend it.

In the 1950s, Brother Andrew smuggled Bibles into communist countries. His prayer was often, "Lord, in my luggage I have Scripture that I want to take to Your children across this border. When You were on earth, You made blind eyes see. Now, I pray, make seeing eyes blind. Do not let the guards see those things You do not want them to see." God worked in amazing ways as guards looked right at the Bibles yet did not see the Bibles and tracts bulging out of his luggage. No difficulty can ever stop God.

George McDonald wrote, "God in His providence has a thousand keys to open a thousand different doors in order to deliver His own, no matter how desperate the situation may have become."

With Peter, the powerful prayers of the early Christians reached our all-powerful God to blind seeing eyes and release Peter from the power of man.

Peter found himself standing outside the prison before he realized what happened. He was still in danger, but he went where the believers were gathered. When he arrived and knocked, a servant-girl heard

Peter's voice, but in her joy, she didn't open the gate but ran to tell the others.

Their response? They said she was out of her mind. They thought it was Peter's angel. They thought he was dead. The believers had been praying, but I wonder what had they prayed? Had their prayers been vague -- asking for God to "be" with Peter, or help Peter, but had they specifically asked for his release? Or did they ask, but didn't really believe?

Peter continued knocking and when they opened and saw him, they were amazed. What God did was amazing, but how sad they didn't expect to be amazed. Are we expecting to be amazed by God?

Throughout the Bible, we read of men and women praying and God working in mighty ways. God continues to work today.

My friend, Emily, founder of The Lulu Tree ministry, traveled to Africa. The team had assembled and prepared birthing kits. Without the simple supplies of a plastic sheet, string, and razor blade, women cannot deliver their babies at a hospital.

Birthing kits and food for 500 had been prepared.

The morning arrived and the number of women seeking help swelled to 800 along with hungry village children. The team prayed and asked God to multiply their supplies.

As Emily and the team watched, God answered

their prayers. Serving dishes somehow refilled and the pile of birthing kits didn't go down. When all had been served, 800 women were miraculously given birthing kits. Even after all had been served, 118 kits were left over. God heard their prayers by blessing and multiplying what they had offered.

God hears the prayers of His children.

In the 1800s George Müller was a thief, liar, and gambler—until God touched his heart. A changed man, Müller began preaching, then felt the call to help poor children. Desiring to show God's faithful provision, not once did he tell anyone of the needs for himself or the ministry. Year after year, day after day, moment by moment, George went only to God in prayer. The result of his faithful prayers? In his lifetime, 117 schools were established which educated over 120,000 children, and through his orphanages, he cared for 18,000 orphans. Eighty-two missionaries were supported, 4,000 Bibles were distributed, and over 1 million tracts and portions of scriptures. The prayer of a righteous person is truly powerful and effective.

Therefore, "do not be anxious or worried about anything, but in everything [every circumstance and situation] by prayer and petition with thanksgiving, continue to make your [specific] requests known to God. And the peace of God [that peace which reassures the heart, that peace] which transcends all understanding, [that peace which] stands guard over your hearts and your minds in Christ Jesus [is yours]." (Philippians 4:6-7, AMP).

Whatever you need, whatever concerns or worries you, go to God. Talk to Him, give Him your concerns. Cast all your cares, all your anxieties, all your worries, and all your concerns, once and for all on Him, for He cares about you with deepest affection, and watches over you very carefully (1 Peter 5:7).

God beckons, *Be still and know that I am God.* Jesus said, "Come to Me, ... and I will cause you to rest. [I will ease and relieve and refresh your souls.] ... and you will find rest (relief and ease and refreshment and recreation and blessed quiet) for your souls" (Matthew 11:28, AMPC).

Coming to God, coming through Jesus to God in prayer we find soul-rest, rest for our minds, and peace that guards our hearts and our minds. Keep praying. For, "Prayer is an all-efficient panoply, a treasure undiminished, a mine which is never exhausted, a sky unobscured by clouds, a heaven unruffled by the storm. It is the root, the fountain, the mother of a thousand blessings." ~ Chrysostom

We are blessed with prayer and praise. God also blesses with His words in the Bible. While reading the first verses of Psalm thirty-seven, several things stood out. We are told to not fret (don't worry) about evil people, and not to get angry and fret because it only leads to evil doing. We are told to trust the Lord, delight in the Lord, commit our way to the Lord, trusting in (and on) Him, leaning on Him, and rolling our worries on Him, and then be still and rest in the Lord.

Along with things we can do, there are things God will do, along with results and promises from God. Would you be willing to look closer at these first verses?

1 **Fret not** yourself because of evildoers, neither be envious against those who work unrighteousness (that which is not upright or in right standing with God). 2 <u>For they shall soon be cut down like the grass</u>, and wither as the green herb.

3 **Trust (lean on, rely on, and be confident) in the Lord and do good**; <u>so shall you dwell in the land and feed surely on His faithfulness, and truly you shall be fed</u>.

4 **Delight yourself also in the Lord,** and <u>He will give you the desires and secret petitions of your heart.</u>

5 **Commit your way to the Lord [roll and repose each care of your load on Him]; trust (lean on, rely on, and be confident) also in Him** and <u>He will bring it to pass. 6 And He will make your uprightness and right</u>

standing with God go forth as the light, and your justice and right as [the shining sun of] the noonday.

7 Be still and rest in the Lord; wait for Him and patiently lean yourself upon Him; fret not yourself because of him who prospers in his way, because of the man who brings wicked devices to pass. **8 Cease from anger and forsake wrath; fret not yourself**—it tends only to evildoing. 9 For evildoers shall be cut off, but those who wait and hope and look for the Lord [in the end] shall inherit the earth. 10 For yet a little while, and the evildoers will be no more; though you look with care where they used to be, they will not be found.

Psalm thirty-seven continues and is filled with hope and encouragement. God knows life is difficult; He understands pain and heartache. Regardless of what we encounter, no matter how evil this world may be, we can trust that God's righteous justice will be served. The things done by wicked people are seen by God and He will punish them for their wicked crimes.

Therefore, fret not. Trust in the Lord, delight yourself in the Lord, lean on Him, be still and rest in His presence.

Look outside your window for a few minutes. What

do you see? For several minutes without looking away, focus on one thing. Now close your eyes. Can you see the imprint of what you were looking at before?

What we see leaves an imprint in our brains. We are advised to "keep and guard your heart with all vigilance and above all that you guard, for out of it flow the springs of life" (Proverbs 4:23, AMPC).

Jesus said, "The good person out of the good treasure of his heart brings forth what is good; and the evil person out of the evil treasure brings forth what is evil; for his mouth speaks from that which fills his heart" (Luke 6:45, NASB). Other translations read "out of the storehouse of the heart." What we see and what we think about matters.

What is being imprinted and stored in our hearts? Jesus, The Life, lives in our hearts. Therefore, we need to, "Guard and keep [with the greatest care] the precious and excellently adapted [Truth] which has been entrusted [to you], by the [help of the] Holy Spirit Who makes His home in us" (2 Timothy 1:14, AMPC).

Guard your heart with where you focus. "Little children (believers, dear ones), guard yourselves from idols— [false teachings, moral compromises, and anything that would take God's place in your heart]" (1 John 5:21, AMP).

Jesus advised, "be on guard so that your hearts are not weighed down and depressed with the giddiness of debauchery and the nausea of self-indulgence and the worldly worries of life, and then that day [when the Messiah returns] will not come on you suddenly like a trap" (Luke 21:34, AMP).

Guard your heart by reading God's Word, which brings understanding of spiritual insight, refreshing, and a boundless wellspring of life (Proverbs 16:22).

Focus and guard your hearts by remembering you "have been chosen of God, holy and beloved, put on a heart of compassion, kindness, humility, gentleness and patience; bearing with one another, and forgiving each other, whoever has a complaint against anyone; just as the Lord forgave you, so also should you. Beyond all these things put on love, which is the perfect bond of unity. Let the peace of Christ rule in your hearts, to which indeed you were called in one body; and be thankful (Colossians 3:12-15, NASB).

Guard your heart from fear, "Say to those with fearful hearts, 'Be strong, do not fear; your God will come, he will come with vengeance; with divine retribution he will come to save you'" (Isaiah 35:4).

Guard your heart by loving the Lord your God with all your heart (Matthew 22:37). Love God with all your heart and your love is forever safe in the One who loves you forever. You are loving Who you can never lose. No one will (and can) snatch your heart out of His loving hand (John 10:28-29).

"If we are obsessed by God, nothing else can get into our lives--not concerns, nor tribulations, nor worries. And now we understand why our Lord so emphasized the sin of worrying. How can we dare to be so absolutely unbelieving when God totally surrounds us? To be obsessed by God is to have an effective barricade against all the assaults of the enemy." ~ Oswald Chambers

Guard your heart by seeking the Lord. "They ... sought Him with all their soul, and He was found by them" (2 Chronicles 15:15). "With my whole heart, I have sought You" (Psalm 119:10). "For the eyes of the Lord move to and fro throughout the earth that He may strongly support those whose heart is completely His" (2 Chronicles 16:9, NASB).

Stay powered up in prayer, powered up in praise, read the Bible meditating on God's truth, and guard your heart by keeping your heart devoted to God.

Fueled and fired up

Our days are measured in increments of time. The Monday morning worker wishes it was Friday. The student longs for the end of the school day. Some spend so much of their time looking at their past that they don't see what is ahead. How do we live in such a way that we remember there is something far better waiting?

Beyond physical sight is an unseen reality. "Things which eye has not seen and ear has not heard, and which have not entered the heart of man, all that God has prepared for those who love Him." (1 Corinthians 2:9, NASB). True life is beyond this earthly life, more real than can be comprehended with our limited understanding.

We are created by God to be here, now, for such a time as this. Each of us has a place in eternity, that lasts for all eternity. We are on mission, left in enemy territory to point to the Savior who sets captives free.

We aren't saved by Christ to be made comfortable. If our goal is an easy life, we will become stagnant and ineffective and will miss the God-given adventure.

Bruce Hurt wrote, "Missio Dei is Latin for 'the sending of God' ... What would happen if all genuine believers truly received a Spirit energized, Word centered, God glorifying vision of their privilege to be 'on mission' with God anywhere and everywhere they were for the rest of their short time on earth?! May God be pleased to raise up many who like Isaiah will be willing to say, 'Here I am. Send me!' (Isaiah 6:8)."

Are we willing to follow wherever our Lord leads? Whether God calls us to serve Him where we are, or follow Him to other places around the world, we are invited to live a God-glorifying, Spirit-energized life.

I tell ya, just thinking about that makes me stand taller. We need to remember who we are in Christ. That each one of us is called with a Holy calling, equipped by the Spirit of God, with the power of God, to be on mission for God.

One night I had a nightmare that an evil man, a demonic man, attacked me, and I took him out. I mean, with ninja-like moves I smacked him down to the ground. Even during the battle, I thought of how I had been raised to be a kind and gentle person, and I probably shouldn't be acting in such a manner, but then I remembered who/what I was fighting, and I fought even harder.

My view of who I was, the truth given through the

power of Christ, was heightened and reminded me of my true identity as a child of God saved by Christ in the power of God and the power of His Son, Jesus Christ.

Amy Carmichael wrote, "We are not called to be weaklings but warriors. So let no one be surprised when the enemy comes in like a flood. But there is no need ever to be overwhelmed. There is not one word in the Bible to tell us to expect to be overwhelmed, for the Spirit of the Lord lifts up a standard against him (Isaiah 59:19) and makes us strong to endure as seeing Him who is invisible."[56]

Therefore, <u>be strong in the Lord drawing your strength from Him and empowered through your union with Him, in the power of His boundless might.</u> <u>Put on the full armor of God which is</u> like the splendid armor of a <u>heavily armed</u> soldier, so that you may be able to <u>successfully</u> stand up against <u>all</u> the schemes and the strategies and the deceits of the devil. For your struggle is not contending only with physical opponents, but against the rulers, against the powers, against the world forces of this present darkness, against the spiritual forces of wickedness in the heavenly supernatural places. Therefore, <u>put on the complete armor of God, so that you will be able to successfully resist and stand your ground</u> in the evil day of danger, and having done everything that the crisis demands, to <u>stand firm</u> in your place, <u>fully prepared, immovable, victorious</u> (Ephesians

6:10-13, using AMP).

With Christ and the Holy Spirit in our lives we are not cream puff weaklings, we are warriors. The armor of God is armor made by God and supplied by God, therefore we (that's you and me!) are given all-mighty, supernatural, custom-fit armor from our almighty God.

Confidence to battle, confidence in battle, comes from confidence in the Lord. For, "the Lord is with me like a dread champion; therefore, my persecutors will stumble and not prevail. They will be utterly ashamed, because they have failed, with an everlasting disgrace that will not be forgotten" (Jeremiah 20:11, NASB 1995).

God's strength and unlimited power are more powerful than any man, any army, any political party, any pandemic, any difficulty faced by humans, and any demonic force in the universe.

God's all-powerful armor is the only armor worthy and able to successfully stand against the supernatural forces of the devil. Therefore, stand firm in <u>God's strength</u>, in <u>God's armor</u>, with the belt of truth, the breastplate of righteousness. Stand firm on the word of God, stand firm on God's truth, stand firm on the good news of the Gospel of peace, the Gospel of Jesus Christ. Stand firm with your shield of faith covering and quenching the flaming missiles of the enemy, and your head covered by the helmet of salvation, and your Sword of the Spirit which is the word of God (Ephesians

6:14-17).

Still, there are times when I've felt like a nail in the board of life being pounded and pounded by all the bad news, heartache, trials, and suffering. One night I tossed and turned in bed worrying and praying when I heard in my spirit, "you have the power of the living God within you; rise up!"

Throughout the Bible, the Spirit of God came upon people to achieve amazing feats. The Holy Spirit gave people the power to prophesy, power to fight and destroy evil, power to withstand terrible trials and persecution, power to speak and share the Gospel, power to do what no ordinary person could do, and the power to live for Christ no matter what was happening in their lives.

As Christians, the Holy Spirit lives within us. Therefore, we can rise up in His power. And, "may the God of your hope so fill you with all joy and peace in believing [through the experience of your faith] that by the power of the Holy Spirit you may abound and be overflowing (bubbling over) with hope" (Romans 15:13, AMPC).

Abounding, overflowing, bubbling over with hope, we can rise up!

The devil <u>will</u> be defeated (is already a defeated foe), and with Christ in your life, in the might of His salvation and strength, <u>you will overcome</u> by your faith in Christ and your testimony. Share what Jesus has done in your life. "Let this be recorded for the generation to come, that a people yet to be created will praise the Lord" (Psalm 102:18, AMP). Therefore, testify about Christ and rise up and rejoice!

No matter what happens, how crazy this world gets, the peace of Christ is in you, therefore, rise up! "Arise, shine; for your light has come, and the glory of the Lord has risen upon you." "knowing that He who raised the Lord Jesus will also raise us with Jesus and will present us [along] with you in His presence" (Isaiah 60:1, NASB; 2 Corinthians 4:14, AMP).

Rise up! You are a warrior, a victorious warrior, empowered by the power of Christ and almighty God. And one day, when your time on earth is done, you will stand before God and hear with the other victorious warriors in heaven "Now salvation, and strength, and the kingdom of our God, and the power of His Christ have come, for the accuser of our brethren, who accused them before our God day and night, has been cast down. And they overcame him by the blood of the Lamb and by the word of their testimony, and they did not love their lives to the death. Therefore rejoice, O heavens, and you who dwell in them!" (Revelation 12:10-12, NKJV).

Speak God's truth, share the good news of the grace of Jesus Christ, for you are here for such a time as this;

rise up! "For if you remain completely silent at this time, relief and deliverance will arise ... from another place, but you and your father's house will perish. Yet who knows whether you have come to the kingdom for such a time as this?" (Esther 4:14, NKJV). No matter how weak you are, no matter how difficult or the length of the battle, rise up.

Jesus said, in this world, you will have trouble. But take heart for He has overcome the world. When Jesus tells us to take heart (take courage), He is reminding us that He has overcome the world. He is **The Champion**! "You see, every child of God overcomes the world, for our faith is the victorious power that triumphs over the world. So, who are the world conquerors, defeating its power? Those who believe that Jesus is the Son of God" (1 John 5:4-5, TPT).

God, your commander, has saved you and called you with a Holy calling (2 Timothy 1:9). You are seated in the heavenlies with Christ (Ephesians 2:6). While your body is still here on earth, you are here to point others to Christ. Therefore, stand firm and rise up!

No matter what we go through on this earth, a happy ending awaits. Therefore, "run with endurance the race God has set before us. We do this by keeping our eyes on Jesus, the champion who initiates and perfects our faith. Because of the joy awaiting him, he endured the cross, disregarding its shame. Now he is seated in the place of honor beside God's throne. Think of all the hostility he endured from sinful people; then you won't become weary and give up" (Hebrews 12:2-2, NLT).

Christ went through an excruciating death on the cross, by keeping His focus on the joy that awaited Him. Christ's joy was knowing His sacrifice would pay the penalty for our sin, and for those who would make Him Lord of their lives they would receive eternal life.

Jesus Christ joyfully went through everything He went through to save you. Stay focused on the big picture, the eternal picture, by remembering the joy set before you, and run to win. "Do you not know that in a race all the runners run [their very best to win], but only one receives the prize? Run [your race] in such a way that you may seize the prize and make it yours! Now every athlete who [goes into training and] competes in the games is disciplined and exercises self-control in all things. They do it to win a crown that withers, but we [do it to receive] an imperishable [crown that cannot wither]" (1 Corinthians 9:24-25, AMP).

Because of persecution, early Christians were scattered to various places. Peter reminded them that even though they were residing as strangers in different lands, they were chosen by God according to His foreknowledge (1 Peter 1:1-3). God chose them to be His, He knew they would be His, and God knew they would be persecuted and scattered.

What did the early Christians do when they were uprooted from their homes, friends, jobs, and probably many of their family members? They told others about Christ. Even when people treated them in horrible ways, they continued to love with God's love and spread the Good News.

"As we look at the saints of old, you might want to ask, what made these saints the kind of saints that they were? It was the intensity of their desire after God. They wanted God more than they wanted anything else. They wanted God more than they wanted ease, comfort, fame, wealth, friends, or even life itself." ~ A. W. Tozer[57]

Jesus said, "If the world hates you, remember that it hated me first. If you belonged to the world, it would love you as it loves its own. But I have chosen you out of the world, so you don't belong to it. That is why the world hates you." (John 15:18-19, NCV).

We have been chosen by Christ, loved by Christ, yet there are those who don't want to hear the truth and want to stop anyone from speaking the truth. Paul warned that all who desire to live godly in Christ Jesus will suffer persecution (2 Timothy 3:12).

"Darkness cannot tolerate light; the more your life illuminates the presence of Christ, the more you should expect opposition from the forces of darkness. Your Christlike nature will be offensive to those in rebellion against Christ's Lordship." ~ Henry and Richard Blackaby[58]

Reading Exodus 1:12 something jumped off the page -- the more the Egyptians afflicted the Israelites, the more they multiplied and the more they spread out.

The more the devil afflicts believers, the more opportunities are given to witness to others. The more trials Christians endure the "What the devil means for evil" God will use for good.

Nik Ripkin, after talking to believers around the world, wrote, "Persecuted believers discovered that the best way to deal with persecutors and to stop their persecution was to pray and witness so that their persecutors would become brothers and sisters in Christ."[59]

Pray for those who persecute you (Matthew 5:44). Pray that God would bless them with salvation.

Don't be surprised at the fiery trials or persecution that comes to test us, as though something strange were happening (1 Peter 4:12). Don't be surprised when life is hard.

"The Lord Jesus made it plain from the beginning that there would be trial of many kinds for all who would follow Him, and He Himself led the way in that path. Should we be surprised when we find ourselves following in His footsteps. ... No one knows what this next year will bring, but one thing is sure. He will be with us, and He is enough for every difficulty that may arise." ~ Amy Carmichael[60]

God's love continues to flow when difficulties come. God is still good when evil people do evil things. Keep remembering the happy ending will come.

Oswald Chambers wrote, "I am convinced that what is needed in spiritual matters is reckless abandonment to the Lord Jesus Christ, reckless and uncalculating abandonment, with no reserve anywhere about it."

"The sadness of today's prevalent attitude in so many situations – 'what do I get out of it?' – is in stark contrast to the attitude of love stirred by the Holy Spirit in a believer's heart – 'what can I give to help in this situation? 'God so loved the world that He gave...' no end, no time limit, no measure, no calculation. His giving could only be called a reckless abandonment of love. Do I love Him in like measure, and am I willing to show it by a similar reckless abandonment?" ~ Helen Roseveare

Will we give the Lord our time, our worship, our focus, and our lives?

"If you would have Christ with you, seek him boldly. Let nothing hold you back. Defy the world. Press on where others flee. ... If Christ be your one and only love, if your heart has cast out all rivals, you will not long lack the comfort of His presence." ~ Charles Spurgeon

"Receive every new day, every new hour, every fresh moment for what it is--a priceless opportunity to be joyfully given in holy love and abandon to Christ, who loved you even to death on the cross. Love-dedicated moments never die--they are caught up to the very throne and heart of God and last eternally, for God is love." ~ Dr. Wesley Duewel

Oh, that we may say "I have one desire now – to live a life of reckless abandon for the Lord, putting all my energy and strength into it." ~ Elisabeth Elliot

Be persistent in prayer, persistent in focusing on Christ, and persistent in your abandonment to God so that you can be used by God for His purpose and glory.

Jesus said, "Ask and keep on asking and it will be given to you; seek and keep on seeking and you will find; knock and keep on knocking and the door will be opened to you" (Matthew 7:7, AMP).

Ask, seek, knock and keep on knocking. Ask the Lord to keep you faithful. Ask the Lord to keep your focus on Him. Keep seeking the Lord. Keep knocking and keep on knocking for the salvation of the lost.

To rid their sin, the Israelites offered burnt offerings and sacrifices on the fire of the altar to God.

"When any one of you brings an offering to the Lord ...burn all on the altar as a burnt sacrifice, an offering made by fire, a sweet aroma to the Lord" (Leviticus 1:1,9, NKJV).

I wonder if when we offer our lives, our hearts, and what we do as service to the Lord, our lives become a sweet aroma to the Lord.

One morning, I was hugged by a friend who had worn a soft, clean perfume. Her gentle fragrance clung to me throughout the day. Taking a deep breath would cause a sweet reminder of that friend. Oh, to be like that perfume, leaving a sweet aroma with the love of Jesus rubbing off onto those we encounter.

"Now thanks be to God who always leads us in triumph in Christ, and through us diffuses the fragrance of His knowledge in every place. For we are to God the fragrance of Christ among those who are being saved and among those who are perishing. To the one we are the aroma of death leading to death, and to the other the aroma of life leading to life." For, "you are God's children whom He loves, so try to be like Him. Live a life of love just as Christ loved us and gave Himself for us as a sweet-smelling offering and sacrifice to God" (2 Corinthians 2:14-16, NKJV; Ephesians 5:1-2, NCV).

As we stay plugged into God's Holy Spirit power-source by steeping ourselves in God's word, spending time with God.

God's wisdom brings internal and external changes. Moses' face shone and beamed from being with, and speaking to, God. "When Moses came down from Mount Sinai with the two tablets of the Testimony in his hand, he did not know that the skin of his face shone and sent forth beams by reason of his speaking with the Lord" (Exodus 34:29, AMPC).

Psalm 34:5 tells us those who look to the Lord are radiant and will never be ashamed. Some translations say we will radiate with joy and no shame will darken our faces. When we live in God's love, we radiate God's love, because we radiate what is inside. We can glow with Christ. We all show the Lord's glory, and we are being changed to be like Him. This change in us brings ever greater glory, which comes from the Lord (2 Corinthians 3:18).

Missionary Adoniram Judson beamed so for Christ that one little boy said he had never seen such a light on any human face, and others called Mr. Judson, "Mr. Glory-face."

Another Christian man was described that his face was a thanksgiving for past mercies and a love-letter to all mankind.

What do people see when they look at us? Are we radiating and beaming with Christ?

At Helen Roseveare's funeral it was said of her, "she was captivated by a glorious goal. She wanted to show Christ that she loved Him and to show the world that Jesus was worthy of that love. No matter what happened in her life, Helen wanted to act in a manner worthy of the Gospel of Christ."[61]

Oh, that those kind words would be said of us. Therefore, "stir up (rekindle the embers of, fan the flame of, and keep burning) the [gracious] gift of God, [the inner fire] that is in you" (2 Timothy 1:6, AMPC).

Stay on fire for God by reading scripture, praying, spending time with God, and keeping your focus on God.

The Israelites were given the Promised Land, yet they had to conquer the evil people who already lived in the land. The Israelites were told, "every place where you set your foot will be yours."

Take ground by moving forward in your faith. Take the ground you have been given by God. Keep going. There is a battle for the souls of the earth, so fight the good fight of faith. Don't allow the enemy to steal your joy, kill your peace, or destroy how God wants to work in your life. God is faithful to complete what He starts. Keep going, don't give up, don't slack off, and don't let the enemy deter your walk in the Lord.

Whatever concerns you, give to God. I had struggled with some things I kept worrying about for over a year. I kept praying, begging for God's help. I whined, lost sleep, and it affected my health. Finally, I went to the Lord and named each issue and told Him, "I can't fix this. I can't stop worrying about this. Father, but You can. Take this issue from me. I put it in Your hands." And, the Lord graciously answered my prayer.

Give your concerns to God. Name them and place them in His hands. Whatever is needed, "God will liberally supply (fill to the full) your every need according to His riches in glory in Christ Jesus" (Philippians 4:19, AMPC).

Count your blessings, name them and remember them. Remember how God rescued His people. Remember what God has done in the Bible, in your own life, and the life of others. Remember He is mighty to save. Remember God's love is unending.

Whatever is done, do for God's glory, making your life a freewill offering to God. Let nothing be done from selfish ambition or empty conceit. God has gifted with salvation, let's gift Him with our lives.

Remember the power of prayer, praise, and thankfulness. Words have the power of life and death, therefore speak life by speaking scripture, singing Psalms and hymns. Let the words of your mouth and the meditation of your heart be acceptable and pleasing in God's sight (Psalm 19:14).

Be brave and strong in the infinite strength supplied by God. Keep your focus on Christ. Remember His promises, and remember He is always with you for now and through eternity (Matthew 28:20).

"Remember, He will never ask you to go where He will not go. He will never ask you to do what He has not done. And He will not ask you to suffer what He has not suffered." ~ A. W. Tozer [62]

Even with all the evil in the world, we are surrounded by God's love and goodness. Please don't let the enemy blind you to the truth—good things do happen, good people do exist, and God's goodness continues working throughout the world.

The Lord is good to all, and His mercy is over all He has made. The Lord is good; His lovingkindness is everlasting, and His faithfulness is to all generations (Psalm 145:9; Psalm 100:5).

The Lord is good and does what is right; He shows the proper path to those who go astray. "The Lord is good, a strength and stronghold in the day of trouble; He knows [He recognizes, cares for, and understands fully] those who take refuge and trust in Him" (Psalm 25:8, Nahum 1:7, AMP).

"For the Lord God is our sun and our shield. He gives us grace and glory. The Lord will withhold no good thing from those who do what is right." And, "We know that for those who love God all things work together for good, for those who are called according to his purpose" (Psalm 84:11, NLT; Romans 8:28, ESV).

"Every good gift and every perfect gift is from above, coming down from the Father of lights, with whom there is no variation or shadow due to change" (James 1:17, ESV).

Oh, taste and see the Lord is good! Blessed is the

one who takes refuge in Him! (Psalm 34:8).

How I want you to know, really know the love of God and the love of His Son, Jesus Christ, "[that you may come] to know [practically, through personal experience] the love of Christ which far surpasses [mere] knowledge [without experience], that you may be filled up [throughout your being] to all the fullness of God [so that you may have the richest experience of God's presence in your lives, completely filled and flooded with God Himself]. Now to Him who is able to [carry out His purpose and] do superabundantly more than all that we dare ask or think [infinitely beyond our greatest prayers, hopes, or dreams], according to His power that is at work within us, to Him be the glory in the church and in Christ Jesus throughout all generations forever and ever. Amen" (Ephesians 3:19-21, AMP).

While you are here on earth, you are here by God's divine plan. Whether you are bedridden, can only crawl, use a wheelchair or walker, or run marathons, you have a purpose in God's amazing plan. Every breath you take, every beat of your heart, means your life continues to have purpose. Your true citizenship lies in Heaven. Therefore, for the joy set before you, keep your eyes on the eternal prize, and run the race the Lord has given you to run.

Love the Lord your God with all your heart, soul,

mind, and strength, and love your neighbor as yourself. Go (as you are going, as you stay where the Lord has placed you), tell others about Christ, and make disciples of the Lord Jesus Christ.

"The very air of heaven is love, for God is love and love never fails. So go on loving not only the loveless but the unlovable, the difficult, the perplexing, the disappointing – unto the end." ~ Amy Carmichael[63]

Float by faith through the storms of life. Float by faith by getting rid of the downdrafts. Float by faith in service to the Lord as you are equipped by the Lord. Float by faith powered up by prayer and thanksgiving. Float by faith fueled up and fired up by the power of the Lord.

Heavenly Father, how I praise You for who You are. Thank You for sending Your Son, Jesus Christ to save us. Thank You, Jesus, for willingly sacrificing Your life in our place for our sins. Father, how I pray to love You with all my soul, mind, and strength. Help me to follow You always.

I pray for the one reading this book that Your love will fall fresh on them. Guide, direct, and bless them to walk with You. May they have a holy excitement as they look to You. Remind them of Your unfailing love. Hold them close through the trials of life. Bless them to remember Your words in scripture that uplift, encourage, and bless their souls.

May we float by faith in Your unending love. May You, Father be glorified, honored, and praised.

We love You Father and ask these things in the name of Your Son, Jesus Christ, who is our Savior. Amen.

Thank you for reading,
Float by Faith

About the author

Lisa Buffaloe is a happily married mom, multi-published author, and speaker. When she's not writing, she enjoys working in her yard, exploring God's beautiful nature, and taking long walks with her sweet husband.

Lisa loves sharing God's unending love and that through Him we find healing, restoration, renewal, and joy.

Visit Lisa at https://lisabuffaloe.com

Books by Lisa Buffaloe

(Updated July 2023)

Non-Fiction
Float by Faith
Heart and Soul Medication
Time with The Timeless One
The Forgotten Resting Place
Present in His Presence
We Were Meant for Paradise
One Lit Step: Devotions for your journey
The Unnamed Devotional
Flying on His Wings
Unfailing Treasures
No Wound Too Deep for The Deep Love of Christ
Living Joyfully Free Devotional, (Volume 1)
Living Joyfully Free Devotional, (Volume 2)

Fiction
The Masterpiece Beneath

Nadia's Hope (Hope and Grace Series, Book 1)
  Prodigal Nights (Hope and Grace Series, 2)
  Writing Her Heart (Hope and Grace Series, 3)
  The Discovery Chapter (Hope and Grace Series, 4)
  Open Lens (Hope and Grace Series, 5)
The Fortune
Grace for the Char-Baked

> I write *"not for professional theologians but for plain persons whose hearts stir them up to seek after God Himself."* ~ A. W. Tozer

Bible credits and Bibliography

The original text of the Bible is rich and full, written in Hebrew, Aramaic, and Greek. The various Bible versions I use during writing are to share the one most appropriate to reveal the beauty and truth of each verse. Some verses are used multiple times to press deep, be cherished, and memorized, the timeless truth of God's word. I gratefully thank each Bible publisher for the use of the scripture quotations.

Scripture taken from the New Century Version® (NCV). Copyright © 2005 by Thomas Nelson, Inc. Used by permission. All rights reserved.

Living Bible (TLB) The Living Bible copyright © 1971 by Tyndale House Foundation. Used by permission of Tyndale House Publishers Inc., Carol Stream, Illinois 60188. All rights reserved.

Scripture quotations taken from the New American Standard Bible®, NASB), Copyright © 1960, 1962, 1963, 1968, 1971, 1972, 1973, 1975, 1977, 1995 by The Lockman Foundation Used by permission. www.Lockman.org

Scripture quotations marked (NLT) are taken from the Holy Bible, New Living Translation, copyright © 1996, 2004, 2007 by Tyndale House Foundation. Used by permission of Tyndale House Publishers, Inc., Carol Stream, Illinois 60188. All rights reserved.

NET Bible® copyright ©1996-2006 by Biblical Studies Press, L.L.C. http://netbible.com

Scripture taken from the New King James Version®. Copyright © 1982 by Thomas Nelson, Inc. Used by permission. All rights reserved.

New American Standard Bible 1995 (NASB1995), New American Standard Bible®, Copyright © 1960, 1971, 1977, 1995 by

The Lockman Foundation. All rights reserved.

Scripture taken from Weymouth translation. Weymouth New Testament. Public domain.

The ESV® Bible (The Holy Bible, English Standard Version®). ESV® Text Edition: 2016. Copyright © 2001 by Crossway, a publishing ministry of Good News Publishers. The ESV® text has been reproduced in cooperation with and by permission of Good News Publishers.

Scripture taken from The Message. Copyright © 1993, 1994, 1995, 1996, 2000, 2001, 2002. Used by permission of NavPress Publishing Group.

Scripture quotations taken from the New Life Version (NLV) Copyright © 1969–2003 by Christian Literature International, P.O. Box 777, Canby, OR 97013. Used by permission.

Scripture quotations taken from the Amplified® Bible (AMP), Copyright © 2015 by The Lockman Foundation Used by permission. www.Lockman.org

Scripture quotations taken from the Amplified® Bible (AMPC), Copyright © 1954, 1958, 1962, 1964, 1965, 1987 by The Lockman Foundation Used by permission. www.Lockman.org

Holman Christian Standard Bible (HCSB) Copyright © 1999, 2000, 2002, 2003, 2009 by Holman Bible Publishers, Nashville Tennessee. All rights reserved.

The Passion Translation®. (TPT) Copyright © 2017 by BroadStreet Publishing® Group, LLC. Used by permission. All rights reserved. ThePassionTranslation.com

---

[1] Cowman, L. B. E.; Reimann, Jim (2008-09-09). *Streams in the Desert: 366 Daily Devotional Readings*, Grand Rapids, MI, Zondervan.
[2] Wiersbe, Warren, *The Bumps Are What You Climb On: Encouragement for Difficult Days*, Grand Rapids, MI, Baker Books
[3] Wubbels, Lance, *Day by Day Through the Gospel of John*, Grand

Rapids, MI, Bethany House Publishers
[4] Tozer, A. W., *Delighting in God*, Grand Rapids, MI, Bethany House Publishers
[5] Smith, James Bryan, *The Magnificent Journey: Living Deep in the Kingdom*, Downers Grove, IL, IVP (An imprint of Intervarsity Press)
[6] Smith, Chuck, *Sermon Notes for Nehemiah 8:9,10*
[7] Carmichael, Amy, *Candles in the dark*, CLC Publications, PA, 2001
[8] Cowman, L. B. E.; Reimann, Jim (2008-09-09). *Streams in the Desert: 366 Daily Devotional Readings*, Grand Rapids, MI, Zondervan.
[9] Roseveare, Helen, *Living Fellowship: Willing to be the third side of the triangle*, Christian Focus Publications
[10] Ibid
[11] Roseveare, Helen, *Living Fellowship: Willing to be the third side of the triangle*
[12] Banks, James, *Prayers for Prodigals: 90 Days of Prayer for your child*, Discovery House, Affiliated with Our Daily Bread Ministries, Grand Rapids, Michigan
[13] Roseveare, Helen, Dr., *Living Sacrifice: Willing to be Whittled as an Arrow*, Christian Focus Publications
[14] Ibid
[15] Cowman, L. B. E.; Reimann, Jim (2008-09-09). *Streams in the Desert: 366 Daily Devotional Readings*, Grand Rapids, MI, Zondervan.
[16] Ibid
[17] Cowman, L. B. E.; Reimann, Jim (2008-09-09). *Streams in the Desert: 366 Daily Devotional Readings*, Grand Rapids, MI, Zondervan.
[18] Miller, J. R., *Making the Most of Life*
[19] Cole, Steven, *Steven Cole sermon*, https://bible.org/seriespage/lesson-70-encouragement-life-s-storms-acts-272-3-21-26-33-36
[20] Simpson, A. B., *Days of Heaven Upon Earth*
[21] Alcorn, Randy, https://www.epm.org/blog/2018/May/9/heavenly-encouragement-race-life
[22] Spurgeon, Charles, *Evening by Evening: faith-building meditations*, New Kensington, PA, Whitaker House
[23] Wubbels, Lance, *Day by day through the Gospel of John*, Minneapolis, MI, Bethany House

[24] Gordon, S. D., *Quiet Talks on Power*
[25] Wiersbe, Warren, *The Bumps Are What You Climb On: Encouragement for Difficult Days*, Grand Rapids, MI, Baker Books
[26] Cowman, L. B. E.; Reimann, Jim (2008-09-09). *Streams in the Desert: 366 Daily Devotional Readings*, Grand Rapids, MI, Zondervan.
[27] Jaynes, Sharon, *Take Hold of the Faith You Long for*, Grand Rapids, Baker Books, 2016
[28] Cowman, L. B. E.; Reimann, Jim (2008-09-09). *Streams in the Desert: 366 Daily Devotional Readings*, Grand Rapids, MI, Zondervan.
[29] Carmichael, Amy, *Candles in the dark*, CLC Publications, PA, 2001
[30] Morgan, Robert J., *Red Sea Rules*, 21
[31] Roseveare, Helen, *Count it all Joy*, Christian Focus Publications, UK
[32] Moody, Dwight, *Trust, Not Feelings*
[33] Israel National News, Miracles in the Six-Day War: Eyewitness Accounts, Eyewitnesses tell the stories of the miraculous battles and events of the Six-Day War. https://www.israelnationalnews.com/news/122435
[34] Cowman, L. B. E.; Reimann, Jim (2008-09-09). *Streams in the Desert: 366 Daily Devotional Readings*, Grand Rapids, MI, Zondervan.
[35] Wubbels, Lance, *Day by day through the Gospel of John*, Minneapolis, MI, Bethany House
[36] Ibid
[37] Blackaby, Henry & Richard, *Experiencing God Day-by-Day: The Devotional and Journal*, B & H Publishing Group, Nashville, TN 997
[38] Wubbels, Lance, *Day by day through the Gospel of John*, Minneapolis, MI, Bethany House
[39] Blackaby, Henry & Richard, *Experiencing God Day-by-Day: The Devotional and Journal*, B & H Publishing Group, Nashville, TN
[40] Ibid
[41] Tozer, A. W., *Delighting in God*, Grand Rapids, MI, Bethany House Publishers
[42] Wubbels, Lance, *Day by Day Through the Gospel of John*, Bethany House, Minneapolis, MN, 2018
[43] Blackaby, Henry and Richard, *Experiencing God Day-by-Day: The Devotional and Journal*, B & H Books
[44] Ibid

[45] Miller, J. R., *Making the Most of Life*
[46] Cowman, Lettie, *Missionary Warrior: Charles E. Cowman*, One Mission Society, Greenwood, IN
[47] Goins, Jeff, *Wrecked: When a Broken World Slams into your Comfortable Life*, Chicago, IL, Moody Publishers, 2012
[48] Gordon, S. D., *Quiet Talks on Power*
[49] Cowman, L. B. E.; Reimann, Jim (2008-09-09). *Streams in the Desert: 366 Daily Devotional Readings*, Grand Rapids, MI, Zondervan.
[50] Tozer, A. W., *We Travel an Appointed Way* (Camp Hill, PA: Christian publications, 1988), 3
[51] Duewel, Wesley L., *Touch the World through Prayer*, Michigan: Zondervan, 1986
[52] Spurgeon, Charles, *Spurgeon on Prayer & Spiritual Warfare*, New Kensington, PA, Whitaker House
[53] Cowman, L. B. E.; Reimann, Jim (2008-09-09). *Streams in the Desert: 366 Daily Devotional Readings*, Grand Rapids, MI, Zondervan.
[54] Shirer, Priscilla, *The Armor of God workbook*, Nashville, TN, Lifeway Women
[55] Currie, Rob, *Hungry for More of God*, AMG Publishers, Chattanooga, TN, 2003
[56] Carmichael, Amy, *Candles in the dark*, CLC Publications, PA, 2001
[57] Tozer, A. W., *No Greater Love*, Bethany House, Minneapolis, Minnesota, 2020
[58] Blackaby, Henry & Richard, *Experiencing God Day-by-Day: The Devotional and Journal*, B & H Publishing Group, Nashville, TN
[59] Nik Ripkin, *The Insanity of Obedience; Walking with Jesus in Tough Places*, B & H Publishing, Nashville, TN
[60] Carmichael, Amy, *Candles in the dark*, CLC Publications, PA, 2001
[61] Roseveare, Helen, *Count it all Joy*, Christian Focus Publications, UK
[62] Tozer, A. W., *No Greater Love*, Bethany House, Minneapolis, Minnesota, 2020
[62] Ibid

Thank you for reading,

Float by Faith
Lisa Buffaloe

www.ingramcontent.com/pod-product-compliance
Lightning Source LLC
Chambersburg PA
CBHW061324040426
42444CB00011B/2762